Introduction

The U.S. Army had experimented late in the First World War with replacing the rear wheels of trucks with the track system of a small commercial tractor. Envisioned as artillery prime movers (towing vehicles), the prototypes were slow, but had improved mobility. Experimentation continued in the immediate post-war period, but no vehicle progressed past the prototype stage.

In 1925, the U.S. Army acquired an unarmoured commercial half-track designed and built by the French firm of Citroën-Kégresse, followed by a larger model in 1931. Both were tested to evaluate their potential as light artillery prime movers. The larger and heavier French half-track weighed 1,955kg (4,300lb). Its 28hp petrol engine provided a top speed of 30kph (18mph) on level paved roads. In the end, both were judged too small and underpowered for the role.

In spite of the U.S. Army's findings, the French Army extensively employed both armoured and unarmoured variants of the Citroën-Kégresse half-tracks during the 1920s and 1930s. The Polish Army, also deploying armoured and unarmoured variants, was the second-largest user in Europe.

After rejecting the French half-tracks, in 1932 the U.S. tested an unarmoured half-track from the American firm of James Cunningham, Son, & Co. It was designated as the Half-Track Car T1. The letter 'T' signified experimental. Larger and heavier than the French vehicles, it weighed 2,865kg (6,300lb) and was powered by a 115hp petrol engine. As with the French half-tracks, the U.S. Army wanted a vehicle suitable for towing light artillery pieces.

Testing the T1 led to some improvements that resulted in a heavier version eventually designated as the T1E1. Thirty were built by the government-owned Rock Island Arsenal, from parts supplied by James Cunningham, Son, & Co. In March 1939, the T1E1 were relabelled as the Half-track Car M1. In December 1940, the secretary of war, a civilian, declared the M1 obsolete, and all disappeared from service.

The unarmoured T1 pilot underwent numerous modifications to improve its performance, which resulted in the new designation as the T1E3. In 1934, it received the vertical volute (coil spring) suspension system (VVSS) developed by the U.S. Army Ordnance Department which proved to be the forerunner of those used on U.S.-built half-tracks during the Second World War.

Volute springs are helically wound steel strips, the inner turns of which are displaced along a central axis to give the finished spring a conical shape. Volute springs have some advantages over other types of tracked suspension systems such as torsion bars because they are more compact and more damage-tolerant. If a portion of volute spring is damaged, the broken pieces can still carry at least part of the original load, something that torsion bars cannot.

Acquired by the U.S. Army in 1931 for test purposes was this unarmoured half-track designed and built by the French firm of Citroën-Kégresse. It received the U.S. Army designation P17 and had front-wheel steering and 22.5-centimetre-wide (9-inch-wide) metal tracks, with attached rubber pads. *Patton Museum*

A single unarmoured pilot of the T1 series, 1934, with a VVSS system. The vehicle later received the designation Half-track Car T1E3. It had fixed rear idlers, which could be adjusted to tighten or loosen the tracks. *Patton Museum*

The U.S. Army pursued the development of a line of unarmoured half-track trucks during the 1930s. Envisioned primarily as artillery prime movers (towing

At the same time as the U.S. Army was testing the unarmoured T1/T1E1, it was also developing larger unarmoured half-tracks trucks, for various roles, from artillery prime movers to perforn role of tank transporter. Their desi ran from Half-track Truck T1 to H Truck T9, eventually designated as track Truck M2.

Design & Development

The Half-track Truck M2 appeared as a light artillery prime mover, with a VVSS system. Initially riding on combination steel and rubber segmented block tracks, like the earlier Half-track Car T1E3, eventually it appeared with something referred to at the time as "endless band tracks". In today's lexicon, endless band track is now just "band track" and often seen on smaller construction and agricultural vehicles.

In 1938, the U.S. Army decided as an experiment to modify the rear body of a Scout Car M3 as pictured and fit it with a version of the vertical volute spring suspension (VVSS) system from the Half-track Truck M2. Notice the gun rail running around the interior of the vehicle with attached machine guns on skates. *Patton Museum*

With a modified version of the VVSS system and the band tracks from the Half-track Truck M2, the converted Scout Car M3 shown became the Half-track Personnel Carrier T7 in 1938. *Patton Museum*

Band track offered some advantages over all-steel tracks at the time. These included a smoother ride with less vibration and therefore less wear on the vehicle, reduced damage to paved surfaces, and greatly increased the service life of a vehicle's bogie wheels and other suspension system components. Band-tracks also weighed approximately 25 percent less than steel-and-rubber segmented block tracks, which improved fuel efficiency and therefore range.

Armoured Half-tracks

In 1938, at the behest of the cavalry branch, the U.S. Army conducted an experiment by converting an existing 4x4 armoured car into an armoured half-track. The cavalry branch wanted an armoured vehicle with superior off-road capabilities to those of its existing wheeled armoured cars. The vehicle chosen for the experiment was a Scout Car M2A1, later re-designated as the M3. The rear wheels of the vehicle were removed, the lower rear hull modified, and a VVSS system from the Half-track Truck M2 fitted, along with 30-centimetre-wide (12-inch-wide) band track.

The much-modified Scout Car M3, with new larger front tyres and weighing 5,530kg (12,170lb), was labelled as the Half-track Personnel Carrier T7. Power came from a 95hp Hercules Motors Corporation petrol engine, which was considered underpowered for the vehicle's weight. The T7 was also eventually provided with an un-ditching roller in place of the original front steel bumper to aid in climbing in and out of shallow ditches.

As with those of the unarmoured Half-track Truck M2, the T7's front wheels were powered and synchronized. This design feature greatly aided off-road performance by giving the driver better steering and the vehicle improved drive-traction. In contrast, the German Army's pre-war half-tracks, both unarmoured and armoured, had unpowered front wheels and depended on their tank-type steering final drive units to turn them past 15° right or left. The unpowered front wheels only supported the front of the vehicle.

The U.S. Army concluded testing the T7 in the same year it began. The vehicle was returned to its original configuration and transferred back to the cavalry branch.

In December 1939, at the request of the artillery branch, which sought a prime mover for its M2 105mm howitzer, the U.S. Army released specifications for an armoured 6,365kg (14,000lb) vehicle designated as the Half-track Scout Car T14. Its design included all experimental and developmental work done on all earlier half-track designs, including the T7. The White Motor Company was assigned the task to build the pilot for testing.

The open-topped T14 pilot vehicle underwent testing in early 1940. The T14 consisted of a specially designed, commercial-type, front and rear drive truck chassis with an armoured hull. Power came from a White 6-cylinder 116hp petrol engine. The T14's VVSS system had front-mounted drive sprockets and rear-mounted idlers. The idlers were fixed in position but were adjustable to increase or decrease band track tension.

In its haste to expand and equip itself in light of the German blitzkrieg in the Ardennes in the summer of 1940, the U.S. Army recommended in September 1940 that the T14 be standardized before the test results were released. It was the invasion of France that brought to the U.S. Army's attention the German Army's employment of an armoured half-track personnel carrier, i.e. the SdKfz 251 Ausf. A. In turn, this prompted U.S. Army interest in a similar vehicle.

The U.S. Army wanted three different modified versions of the T14 rushed into production for its armoured divisions. Manufacture of these vehicles received official approval in October 1940. They would include the Half-track Car M2, the 81mm Mortar Carrier M4 (based on the Half-track Car M2) and the Half-track Personnel Carrier M3.

The M2/M3 series half-tracks may not have been the optimum choice for the U.S. Army's needs at that time. Their lack of overhead protection as well as thin armour would prove unpopular with those who served in them. But, it was simple in design as it employed many commercial truck components that brought down cost and tooling effort and lead time, thus allowing it to be built by American industry in very large numbers relatively quickly. In that time frame, a half-track cost approximately $14,000 to build compared to a tank, which cost approximately $35,000.

All three modified versions of the T14 were powered by the same six-cylinder White 147hp petrol engine, which provided a power to weight ratio of approximately 15hp per ton. The current U.S. Army M1A2 Abrams main battle tank, which weighs over 70 tons, has a power to weight ratio of 21.4hp per ton.

The new half-tracks had a respectable top speed of 75kph (45mph) on level paved roads. Off-road speed was dictated by

In December 1939, the U.S. Army authorized the construction of the Half-track Scout Car T14 pilot pictured. In the name of expediency, the pilot vehicle had the Half-track Personnel Carrier T7's vertical volute spring suspension (VVSS) system , as well as band tracks, and front-mounted roller. *Patton Museum*

In October 1940, the U.S. Army ordered three modified (but generally similar versions) of the Half-track Scout Car T14. One of the three, seen here, received the designation Half-track Car M2. A spotting feature was the large ammunition storage compartment doors behind the driver's compartment on either side of the vehicle. *Patton Museum*

The U.S. Army took notice of the German Army's use of half-track armoured personnel carriers during its conquest of France in the summer of 1940. The vehicle then in use is pictured and bore the designation SdKfz. 251 Ausf. A. Armed with two machine guns, it transported a squad of ten men. *Patton Museum*

The Half-track Car M2 lacked a rear door as evident in this picture of several being shipped on railcars. The metal enclosures on the bottom rear of the vehicle contained brake lights and taillights. *National Archives*

Coming off the production line in the same month as the Half-track Car M2, i.e., May 1941, is the Half-track Personnel Carrier M3 pictured. The M3 lacked the large ammunition storage compartments seen on either side of the M2 and its troop compartment was 25 centimetres (10 inches) longer. *Patton Museum*

Shown is the standard chassis of the M2/M3 half-tracks, with its vertical volute spring suspension (VVSS) system and band tracks. Unlike the Half-track Scout Car T14, which had a rear-mounted drive sprocket and front-mounted idler, the M2/M3 series, had the positions reversed. *Patton Museum*

the type of terrain traversed. Chains were provided for the band tracks and front tyres to aid in travelling over mud and snow. For the front wheels, there were semi-elliptic longitudinal leaf springs. More durable front springs began phasing-in to M2/M3 production in May 1943. The front wheels also had hydraulic brakes as did the vehicle's VVSS system's two drive sprockets.

The band tracks fitted to the half-track were made by vulcanizing rubber over steel cables for added strength and durability. The two separate strands in the band tracks were joined together by steel cross pieces, which included small rectangular steel-framed openings. These openings were engaged by the tracks' drive-sprockets' 18 interior teeth, which in turn, pulled the band tracks from the rear of the vehicle and laid them down in front of the advancing suspension system assemblies. Also, the steel cross pieces had attached steel guide teeth that aided in keeping the tracks aligned on the VVSS system.

The rubber-tyred bogie wheel assemblies on either side of the vehicle's rear hull, were fitted with two vertical volute springs each, which supported most of the vehicle's weight. The volute springs were not visible because they were inside protective steel coverings referred to as the volute suspension brackets. New heavier and more durable bogie springs began appearing on the M2/M3 production lines in May 1942. Due to a serious rubber shortage, beginning in July 1943, new M2/M3 half-tracks began rolling off the production lines with synthetic rubber band tracks and bogie wheels.

Located on the top of each of the vehicle's volute suspension bracket on either side wof the vehicle was a single attached rubber-tyred return roller. The return rollers supported and carried the upper portion of the band tracks as the drive sprockets pulled the tracks forward.

From a wartime U.S. Army publication titled the *Basic Half-track Vehicles M2, M3 Technical Manual* appears this warning about not overloading the vehicles: "The vehicle must be carefully loaded. Excessive breaking of springs has been a constant source of trouble in the vehicles used in the desert. The rough going is very hard on springs, and they are quickly broken by overloading, improper distribution of load, or shifting of load while moving."

Access to the engine was by way of two folding hinged armoured top and side panels on either side of the engine compartment, which were attached to a fixed centre armour panel. Small latches on either side of the engine compartment held them in place. When raised, the folding armoured top and side panels lay on top of the fixed centre armour panel. To remove the engine required an overhead hoist to lift off the fixed centre armour panel.

As with commercial trucks of the day, the M2/M3 half-tracks had a manually operated transmission. Those on the half-tracks came from the Spicer Manufacturing Company. The transmission provided four forward speeds and one reverse gear. The half-track's front axles were also a Spicer product. Power for the M2/M3 half-track drive sprockets came from a drive shaft from the engine, which connected to a differential housing located between the drive sprockets.

The maximum grade the M2/M3 half-tracks could overcome was 60 percent. They were supposed to be able to climb over a 30-centimetre (12-inch) vertical wall and have a fording depth of 80 centimetres (32 inches). Like the T14, the M2/M3 half-tracks used 30-centimetre-wide band track.

With fuel capacity for 270 litres (60 gallons) in two self-sealing 135-litre (30-gallon) tanks, the M2/M3 half-tracks had a cruising range of approximately 280 kilometres (175 miles). The tanks on the M2 were in the rear of the troop compartment on either side. Those on the M3 were on either side of the front of the troop compartment, behind the driver's and vehicle commander's seats. For extinguishing onboard fires, a single two-pound portable carbon dioxide fire extinguisher was provided.

The M2/M3 half-tracks were protected by face-hardened armour (FHA) plates screwed together. FHA was normal steel armour plate put through an extra heating process to harden its outer surface while retaining the toughness of the original armour plate. The process allowed FHA to break up attacking projectiles of a certain calibre that impacted its extremely hard surface, thereby greatly reducing penetration. The downsides of FHA are that it is difficult to manufacture, which makes it more expensive, and it has limited shock resistance to overmatching projectiles and fragments due to its inherent brittleness.

The 12.7mm-thick armoured windshield cover of the M2/M3 half-tracks was attached to three hinges at the top of the vehicle's windshield frame. In its open raised position, it projected horizontally over the shatterproof glass windshield and was supported by three small upright steel rods.

Before entering combat, the two-section shatterproof glass windshield of the M2/M3 came off. The three small upright steel support rods went into indentations on the vehicle's armoured engine bonnet, and the armoured windshield then lowered into place. It had two small rectangular direct vision slots that could be covered by armour flaps raised and lowered by the driver and assistant driver when required by small turn screws.

The radiator at the front of the M2/M3 half-tracks was protected by four horizontal armoured shutters 6.4mm thick, which could be opened or closed by the driver from within the vehicle. The armoured shutters had three intermediate positions set by the driver. The remainder of the half-track also received protection from FHA with a thickness of 6.4mm. The half-track's armour was intended to stop 7.62mm

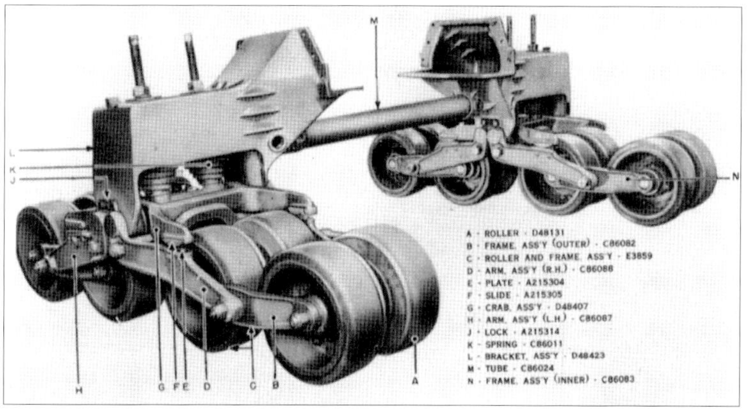

The rubber-tyred metal bogie wheels seen in this image from an M2/M3 series manual first appeared on the Half-track Scout Car T14. Also visible are the bottom portions of the two volute springs mostly hidden from view by the bracket assemblies on each side of the suspension system. *Patton Museum*

Taking part in a training exercise held in the United States in November 1941 is a Half-track Car M2. Notice the inner gun rail inherited from the Scout Car M3. *National Archives*

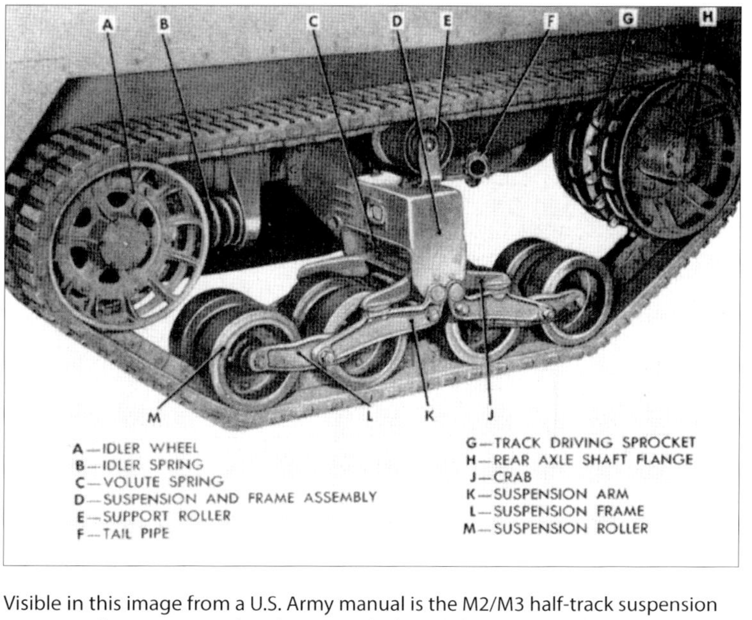

Visible in this image from a U.S. Army manual is the M2/M3 half-track suspension system with components listed. Among the listed objects is the idler spring, which started appearing on all new production M2/M3 half-tracks in September 1942. *Patton Museum*

The International Harvester Company (IHC) also received a contract to build a copy of the Half-track Car M2. With the approval of the Ordnance Department, they made it identical to their own Half-track Personnel Carrier M5A1, with only the configuration of the troop compartment differing. The vehicle received the designation Half-track Car M9A1. *TACOM*

Leaving the White factory located in Cleveland, Ohio in June 1941 are Half-track Car M2s. Notice the hinged upper portion of the driver's door has been lowered, and in its place is a small tarp with a clear plastic insert. *National Archives*

armour-piercing (AP) bullets at a horizontal range of 185 metres (200 yards).

In comparison, the German SdKfz. 251 armoured personnel carrier series had 8mm of sloped armour providing a higher degree of protection for its passengers; however, the SdKfz's sloped armour provided less internal storage compared to the American half-track's. The German half-track's front nose plate over the radiator had a thickness of 14.5mm.

Testing and initial field use of the new M2/M3 half-tracks uncovered that the vehicle's fixed rear idlers, adjustable for track tension, worked well on roads. However, once off-road, the fixed rear idlers proved unable to compensate for the increased movement of the VVSS components, resulting in thrown band tracks or damage to suspension system components.

The solution came from two bright young men of the U.S. 2nd Armoured Division in the spring of 1942. At their commander's expense, they fashioned a pair of jury-rigged coil-spring-loaded idlers, which they fitted to a half-track in place of its original fixed idlers. Testing quickly demonstrated that they had solved the problem, as the springs provided 'give' on rough terrain, but quickly took up slack.

Eventually, the 2nd Armoured Division commander, Major General Ernest N. Harmon approved of the quick-fix device, and all the division's half-tracks were so equipped. The U.S. Army's Chief of Ordnance quickly approved it as a field modification in July 1943 for all those half-tracks built before that time. It later became a standard-factory-applied part.

The Builders

Due to anticipated requirements for a large number of half-tracks, the U.S. Army concluded in September 1940 that no single firm could build the number required. Therefore, three firms were selected to build the half-tracks: White, the Autocar Company, and the Diamond T Motors Company, all heavy-truck manufacturers.

By standardizing parts, across both types and all three manufacturers, manufacturing would be faster and at lower cost, and maintenance and logistics greatly simplified. For example, all were powered by the same White Motors six-cylinder inline engine.

White was in existence from 1900 to 1980, building a wide variety of wheeled vehicles, from cars to trucks over the many decades it was in business. The Autocar Company was founded in 1897 and acquired by White in 1953. The Diamond T Motor Company, founded in 1905, came under the ownership of White in 1958 and lasted as a separate marque until 1966. White and Autocar built the M2, whereas all three firms built the M3.

Following the Japanese attack on Pearl Harbor in December 1941, which officially brought the United States into the Second World War, the conclusion came about in February 1942 that even more half-tracks would be required to satisfy the U.S. Army needs, and United States Government Lend-Lease commitments to wartime allies for military equipment.

The original forecast of half-tracks needed by the U.S. Army by 1944 totalled 188,404 units. Broken down, this called for 21,938 units to be delivered by the end of 1942, another 123,714 by the end of 1943, and the remaining 42,752 units by the end of 1944. In June 1942, the number of half-tracks was revised, resulting in a minor drop in numbers. The new requirement called for 21,653 units by the end of 1942, 63,471 units by the end of 1943, and 101,458 units by the end of 1944, for a total of 186,582 units.

The July 1943 TO&E (table of organization and equipment) for a U.S. Army infantry division called for only three trailer-towing

Half-track Personnel Carriers M3/M3A1s in the division's Cavalry Reconnaissance Troop. Wartime pictorial evidence shows that an unknown number of the infantry divisions that served in the European Theatre of Operation (ETO) had replaced their 1½-ton 6x6 trucks as prime movers for their 57mm anti-tank guns with surplus Half-track M2/M2A1s. If this proved to be the case for all three infantry regiments of an infantry division, then their modified TO&E would indicate there were 54 additional half-tracks in their vehicle inventory.

To meet the required numbers deemed necessary in 1941, the U.S. Army brought in a fourth manufacturer, the International Harvester Company (IHC). The IHC-built half-tracks incorporated the lessons learned from the U.S. Army's testing and field use with the earlier M2/M3 half-tracks. The result was the IHC half-track had an IHC-built petrol engine producing up to 143hp, new front tyre design, heavier springs, and axles fitted plus a host of other improvements.

The most dramatic change in design with the IHC-built half-tracks was the switch from the screwed-together FHA plates employed in the construction of half-tracks by the original three builders to rolled homogenous armour (RHA) plates welded together.

Homogeneous armour is essentially uniformly hard throughout its depth and has a very high degree of ductility (the property of a material that allows it to withstand large amounts of deformation before fracturing). It is therefore not only easier and more cost-effective to make than FHA but also lends itself more easily to machining and arc welding.

The possibility of employing RHA plates welded together for the construction of future half-tracks first appeared in 1941. To test the concept both an M2 and M3, constructed of RHA rather than FHA, were subjected to live-fire testing. The trials revealed that the welded-together RHA side plates eliminated the seams through which bullet-splash occurred and lacked the cap screws that were driven into FHA-equipped half-tracks when struck.

A downside of the RHA plates was that their ballistic resistance was a bit less when compared to FHA of the same thickness. To compensate the U.S. Army decided that the thickness of RHA of IHC-built half-tracks would be increased to the point that it offered the same ballistic protection afforded by the M2/M3 half-tracks' FHA protection. As a result, the maximum armour thickness on the vehicles would rise to 15.9mm on its armoured windshield cover, with the rest of vehicle's armour being 7.9mm thick. Approval for RHA to be incorporated in the construction of the future IHC half-tracks appeared in 1942.

To oversee the companies the Ordnance Department of the U.S. Army formed the Half-Track Integrating Committee in September 1942. Its role was to coordinate the builders' production and manage phase-in of the many design changes and requirements changes. Unlike some problem-plagued procurement programmes, such as heavy trucks, the production of half-tracks posed no unusual issues for the builders or the Ordnance Department.

The U.S. Army did not want to mix the IHC-built half-tracks with the existing inventory of M2/M3 series half-tracks. The majority of the IHC half-tracks therefore were allocated for Lend-Lease, with the bulk going to the British Army, with 5,238 units delivered.

As the British Army already had a full-tracked armoured personnel carrier, the Universal Carrier, there was no pressing requirement for the M5/M5A1. The British Army, therefore, transferred a great many to either Commonwealth armies, or other Allied forces under British Army oversight. Those IHC-built half-tracks retained by the British Army were employed as personnel carriers, artillery prime movers, or as general-purpose utility vehicles by engineering units.

The second-largest Lend-Lease recipient of the American half-tracks proved to be the Free French who acquired approximately 2,000 units, consisting of both IHC-built half-tracks and those built by the original three American builders.

The Red Army received approximately 1,200 American-built half-tracks, also consisting of IHC-built half-tracks and those built by the original three American manufactures. The great majority were employed as prime movers with the Red Army. Some of the Lend-Lease half-tracks provided to the Red Army found themselves passed on to the Polish People's Army.

As events transpired, the number of half-tracks required by the U.S. Army following the attack on Pearl Harbor in December 1941 had been greatly overestimated. An important factor was the reduction of the number of armoured divisions to be formed by the U.S. Army, which fell from a high of 61 to only 16 by the summer of 1943.

As the majority of M2/M3 half-tracks procured were intended for the U.S. Army's armoured divisions, their drop in numbers caused a corresponding decrease in the number of half-tracks eventually needed. In October 1943, the U.S. Army revised downward the number of half-tracks it envisioned requiring. From the original high of 188,404 units anticipated in February 1941, the number required dropped to a total of 87,303 units by the end of 1944. In the end, by June 1945, when the last half-tracks came off the assembly lines, approximately 54,000 units had been completed. The first production M2s rolled off the White assembly lines in May 1941, with Autocar's arriving the following month. When M2 production ended in September 1943, a total of 11,415 had come off the assembly lines, with the majority built by White.

M2/M3 in Detail

The early-production M2/M3 half-tracks had a fixed headlight on either front fender. These were protected by fixed brush guards that included a small blackout marker light for travelling in convoy at night. Because the fixed fender-mounted headlights were prone to shattering from muzzle blast on those M3s armed with field guns or howitzers, new dismountable headlights behind a new brush-guard design appeared.

Pictured is the original fixed fender-mounted headlight and brush-guard design for the M2/M3 half-tracks. Due to the damage caused by the muzzle blast of artillery weapons fitted to some M3 half-tracks, the U.S. Army replaced the fixed headlights with dismountable headlight with brush guard. *Patton Museum*

Visible is the replacement two-piece combination headlight and brush guard for M2/M3 half-tracks. It fitted into a mounting bracket attached to either side of the forward engine compartment and began appearing on the production lines in November 1942. *Patton Museum*

The new dismountable headlights began appearing on all production M2/M3 half-tracks beginning in November 1942. In June 1943, a Modification Work Order (MWO) went out to retrofit all earlier half-tracks armed with field guns or howitzers with the dismountable headlights.

The one-piece dismountable headlights included a blackout marker light and brush guard. They attached to a fixed mounting bracket on either side of the engine compartment on the half-tracks so fitted and were secured in place by a locating plunger at the back of the bracket.

The M2 had an approximate length of 6 metres (19 feet 6 inches) with a front-mounted roller. Fitted with a front-mounted winch, it came out to about 6.1 metres (20 feet and 1 inch). The winch had a capacity of 4,550kg (10,000lb). When fielded with a front-mounted roller the M3 had an approximate length of 6.2 metres (20 feet 3 inches) and 6.3 metres (20 feet 9 inches) with a front-mounted winch. Essentially, without the front-mounted rollers and winches, both vehicles were about the same length.

The major difference was that the M3 was intended to carry a 12-man infantry squad, and therefore had a longer troop compartment that seated ten men. The M2 could only carry eight men in its shorter rear troop compartment. Unlike the M3, the M2 had two horizontal assemblies on the lower rear external face of their troop compartments, which contained the vehicle's taillights.

The Half-track Car M2 pictured has the side mine racks that began appearing on the M2/M3 half-track production lines in August 1942. It also has the new dismountable combination headlight and brush guard. *Patton Museum*

Both half-tracks had a height of 2.26 metres (7 feet 5 inches) and width of 1.96 metres (6 feet 5¼ inches). With the later addition of mine racks on either side of their rear compartments, their width increased to 2.3 metres (7 feet 5¼ inches). The M2 weighed 9,000kg (19,800lb) and the 9,090kg (M3 20,000lb).

The M2 fulfilled three different interim roles: artillery prime mover, reconnaissance vehicle, and light machine-gun-squad-transport vehicle in armoured infantry platoons of armoured divisions. It assumed these various interim roles as there was nothing else then available. It would take time for American industry to design and

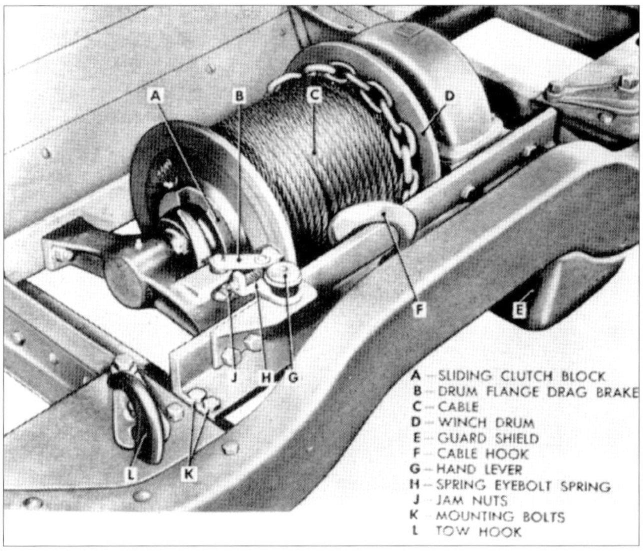

The M2/M3 half-track series also appeared with the front-mounted Tulsa Model 18G winch pictured, instead of the front-mounted roller. Power for the winch came from the vehicle's transmission. *Patton Museum*

The various visible radio antennas indicate that this particular early-production Half-track Car M2 is a reconnaissance vehicle. Just in front of the right-hand-side headlight assembly is a small licence plate with the letters APG, which stand for Aberdeen Proving Ground. *Patton Museum.*

The Half-track Car M2 pictured is armed with two .50-calibre machine guns. Notice the improvised wooden storage box on the rear of the vehicle, which had the crew relocate the weapon's ground tripods to the right front fender. *Patton Museum*

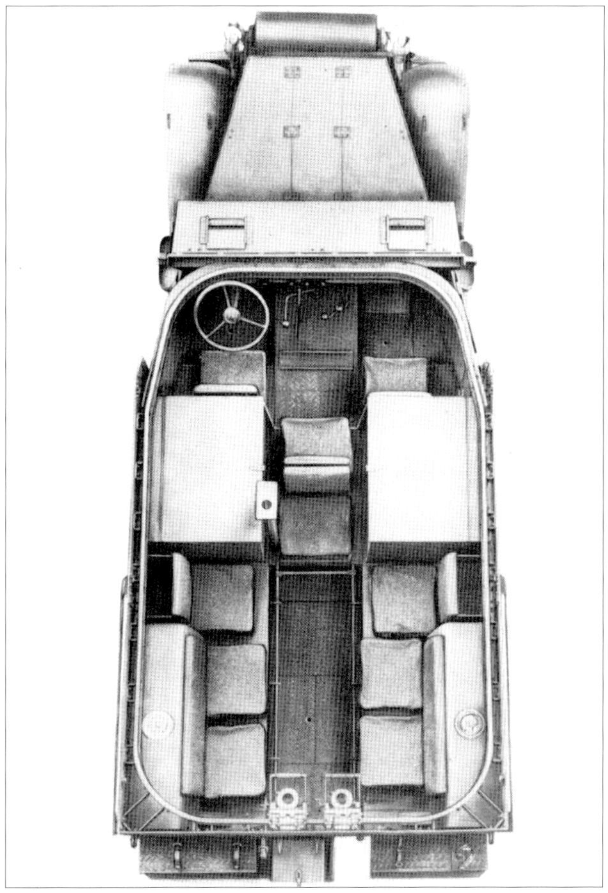

The two ammunition storage compartments of the Half-track Car M2 appear in this photograph as well as the two 30-gallon fuel tanks. Also visible is the gun rail that ran around the inside of the vehicle, on which movable skates slid. It was the skates to which machine guns and their pintles attached. *Patton Museum*

The driver's compartment of a Half-track Car M2A1. The appearance and configuration was almost the same for the entire M2/M3 series and variants. Notice the 2lb portable fire extinguisher in the foreground. *Patton Museum*

The Half-track Car M2 lacked a rear door because of its primary role as an artillery prime mover. The difficulty of entering or leaving the vehicle over the attached trails of the artillery piece is evident from the photograph. *Patton Museum*

build all the different types of specialized vehicles required.

As an interim artillery prime mover, the M2 came with two large ammunition storage compartments on either side of the vehicle located directly behind the driver's and commander's positions. These opened from the outside of the vehicle but projected into the rear passenger area of the vehicle. The compartments also opened inside the vehicle via an overhead hatch that allowed access to the top rack of ammunition.

The Half-track Car M2's original armament called for a single air-cooled .50-calibre machine gun and two water-cooled .30-calibre machine guns. The fixed headlight and the absent mine rack, mean this vehicle was built before August 1942. *TACOM*

In this photograph, we see the horizontally stored tripod for the onboard .50-calibre machine gun on the rear of a Half-track Car M2. Also visible in the lower left-hand-side metal enclosure is the covered electrical outlet for powering the brake lights on towed artillery pieces or trailers. *National Archives*

Two of the vehicle's ten-man crew sat back to back in between the two ammunition storage compartments. The other six sat in two rows of three seats behind the ammo storage compartments, down the length of the vehicle, facing each other. The M2 driver sat in the left front of the vehicle and the squad leader to his right.

The M2's initial authorized armament consisted of a single .50-calibre M2 heavy barrel (HB) air-cooled machine gun, and two water-cooled .30-calibre M1917A1 machine guns. These weapons were mounted on a gun rail that circled the crew compartment and gave a wide field of fire. For dismounted use, there were three tripods stowed on the rear plate of the troop compartment.

By war's end, American industry had built approximately 350,000 units of the .50-calibre M2 heavy barrel (HB) air-cooled machine gun. About 70,000 units of the water-cooled .30-calibre M1917A1 machine guns were built during the First World War and an additional 50,000 during the Second World War.

Eventually, the two water-cooled .30-calibre machine guns were replaced by a single air-cooled .30-calibre M1919A4 machine gun and one tripod was eliminated. Authorized ammunition storage on board the M2 was 700 rounds of .50-calibre ammunition and 7,750 rounds of .30-calibre ammunition. Because of the gun rail, the M2 had no rear door, requiring those in the troop compartment to climb over the vehicle's sides.

In addition to the authorized machine-gun ammunition, the M2 normally carried ten hand grenades and when fitted with external mine racks (approved in August

1942) on either side of the vehicle's rear troop compartment, up to 14 units of the Mine, Anti-tank, High-Explosive, M1A1. The latter could be set to detonate at either 250lb or 500lb (115kg or 230kg) of pressure on the striker head of the mine. In February 1943 a modification work order went out that authorized the installation of mine racks on all half-tracks built before August 1942.

In this picture of we see a private collector's early-production Half-track Car M2, identified as such by the fixed fender-mounted headlights. Inboard of the headlight on the left-hand fender is a seldom-seen fixed blackout light attached to the engine compartment. *Pierre Oliver Buan*

Communications

The communication methods available to an armoured infantry battalion appear in a November 1944 manual titled *Armoured Infantry Battalion*:

"Communication facilities of the armoured infantry battalion are radio, wire, messenger, visual and sound signals, and pigeons. The battalion commander in planning communication to be used under various conditions, considers the capabilities and limitations of each available means of communication, selecting the method best suited to the situation. Alternate means are always provided. The battalion commander is responsible for having available at all times two or more means of communication with higher headquarters, subordinate and adjacent units."

Each of the rifle platoon leader's half-tracks had an SCR-510 FM (frequency modulated) radio to tie in with the company's SCR-510 and SCR-528 FM radio sets. Considered a medium-range radio set, the SCR-510 had an approximately 75-mile reach when employing Morse code, and a 25-mile reach for voice.

Visible on the rear right-hand side of the Half-track Personnel Carrier M3A1 is a radio set. Not all M3/M3A1s had onboard radios. Usually in an armoured infantry platoon of five vehicles only the platoon commander's vehicle was equipped with a built-in radio set. Notice the hand grips below the seat cushions, which began appearing on the production lines in July 1942. *TACOM*

The SC-528 ranked as a short-range radio set, with a maximum reach under optimum conditions of ten miles for voice only. The estimated range of the radio sets then in use were often influenced by the time of day, weather, and terrain features.

The U.S. Army was a pioneer in the development of FM radio sets for short-range tactical communications, unlike the German Army that relied on AM radio sets for its tanks and other armoured vehicles throughout the Second World War.

For dismounted use, the platoon leader's vehicles had an SCR-300 FM backpack radio, best known by its wartime nickname as the 'walkie-talkie'. The other four half-tracks in an armoured infantry rifle platoon did not have vehicle-mounted FM radios. Rather, one half-track per platoon had an SCR-536 hand-held AM radio, best known by its popular nickname as the 'handie-talkie'.

Because the SCR-536 handie-talkie was an AM radio, it could not communicate with U.S. Army tanks that only had FM radios. A quick fix involved providing spare SCR-536 handie-talkies to the crews of medium tanks. Another short-term solution involved affixing an EE-8 field telephone onto the rear of a medium tank hull, connected to the tank's intercom system. This was first implemented in the field in July 1944 and remained in use until the end of the war.

The eventual solution for providing a means by which the dismounted armoured infantry could remain in radio contact with their tank counterparts was to install a modified version of the AM SCR-536 handie-talkie, labelled as the AN/VRC-3, into the headquarters' tanks of each tank company as well as one tank per five-tank platoon. This process began in September 1944 and was completed by December 1944.

Reflecting the differences in design and construction materials utilized by IHC in building their half-track variants, they were assigned new designations. The M2/M3 versions built by IHC respectively became the M9A1 and M5. The M5A1 eventually followed the M5 and featured the same M49 machine-gun ring mount over the right front of the vehicle as seen on the M2A1 and the M3A1. The usage of RHA on the IHC-built half-tracks caused a slight weight increase but only marginally compromised their performance compared to those built of thinner FHA.

Standing in the rear troop compartment of a Half-track Car M9A1 and looking forward we see at least two radio sets and the antenna mast for one of them in the foreground. There is a metal storage compartment visible on the right that did not open to the outside as it did on the Half-track Car M2/M2A1 and 81mm Mortar Carriers M4/M4A1. *TACOM*

When the Half-track Car M2 lost favour with the artillery branch as a prime mover, its primary role was as a reconnaissance vehicle. This change in roles is evident in this M2A1 which has had its left-hand-side ammunition storage compartment replaced by a platform shelf for an SCR-528 radio set. *Chris Hughes*

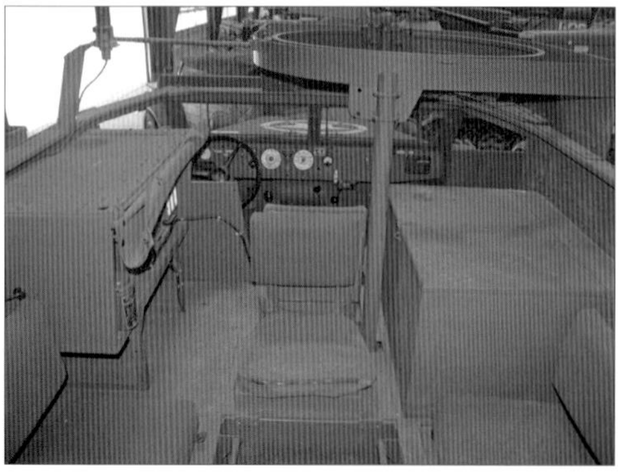

In this photograph of a Half-track Car M2A1, we can see an SCR-528 radio set has replaced the vehicle's left-hand-side ammunition storage compartment. A cable from the top of the radio attaches to a nine-foot whip antenna. Notice that the right-hand-side ammunition storage compartment has been cut back in this photograph. *TACOM*

As with the M2/M3, at a certain point, the thought of combining the M9A1 and the M5 into only a single model was discussed. The only pilot was assigned the designation Half-track Car T31, with production set to begin in March 1944; however, at that time, the U.S. Army had already ended all new half-track production contracts. The rebuilding of those that had been employed in training duties in the United States and then shipped overseas satisfied all existing requirements.

The employment of RHA with the IHC-built half-tracks resulted in an easily identified external design feature, as the rear corners of the vehicles were rounded, rather than the squared corners of those half-tracks built of FHA. Another external design feature specific to the IHC-built half-tracks was a simple curved flat steel stamping employed for the front fenders, whereas those seen on the half-tracks built from FHA were more elaborate and traced their roots back to commercial truck fenders.

Unlike the M2/M2A1, the corresponding IHC M9A1 was a bit different, in that it was provided with a rear passenger compartment door and was the same length as the M5/M5A1. Deleted from the M9A1 design were the lower side doors on either side of the vehicle, directly behind the driver's compartment, as seen on the M2/M2A1. This design change and the added length of the M9A1 makes it difficult to distinguish from the M5A1, without reference to their respective internal arrangements.

In total IHC built 11,017 units of their copies of the M2/M3 half-track series between December 1942 and March 1944. The breakdown is 3,433 units of the M9A1, 4,625 units of the M5, and 2,959 units of the follow-on M5A1. Approximately 4,000 units of the IHC-built half-tracks went through a remanufacturing process between July 1944 and June 1945 after hard use.

As with the Half-track Car M2 and Half-track Personnel Carrier M3, the Half-track Personnel Carrier M5 eventually appeared with the M49 ring mount and received the designation M5A1. Instead of the rounded commercial type front fenders seen on the M2/M3 series half-tracks, the M5 and M5A1 had flatter front fenders. *TACOM*

M2/M3 Variants

The M2A1 replaced the M2, with 1,643 units built between October 1943 and March 1944. An additional 1,266 units of the M2 were upgraded to the M2A1 configuration between January 1944 and June 1945. The external identifying feature of the M2A1 was the added armoured M49 ring mount located over the right-hand front passenger seat. The ring mount had been authorized in May 1943 and was normally armed with a .50-calibre machine gun, replacing the gun rail. However, a rear door was not added.

With the deletion of the gun rail, three fixed pintle sockets were fixed on the left, right, and rear sides of the rear passenger compartment. The combination of pintle and ring mounts addressed a tactical weakness in the gun rail mounts—bringing a weapon to bear on a threat from a new direction. With the added armoured ring mount the M2A1's height increased to 2.7 metres (8 feet 10 inches).

In trying to improve the operational parameters of the M2 the U.S. Army came up with an experimental version in early 1942 designated as the Half-track Car T16. It had a lengthened frame, and an enlarged VVSS system fitted. The engine and powertrain remained the same as the standard M2.

The new half-track suspension system fitted to the T16 came with larger rubber-tyred bogie wheels, and 35.6-centimetre-wide (14-inch-wide) band tracks with increased ground contact. These design features were anticipated to reduce the vehicle's ground pressure, which would improve its off-road mobility.

In the vernacular of the time, the ground pressure went by the term floatation. The term did not imply the ability to float in water, but the perceived ability of a military vehicle to float over 'soft' terrain. However, the T16's design included a 6.4mm-thick raised armoured roof for crew protection, which with the longer and heavier frame, reduced vehicle performance to such an extent that the programme was cancelled.

In December 1942 the U.S. Army considered rationalizing half-track manufacture by replacing the M2 and M3 with a new version based on the M3, whose interior configuration would vary based on role. Only a single pilot vehicle was built to test the concept, originally designated the Half-track Car T29 and later as the Half-track Car M3A2. However, by early 1944 requirements for half-track cars were significantly reduced, and all manufacturing cancelled. More M3s where in inventory than needed, so the M3A2 project ended.

The artillery branch, unhappy with the limited off-road mobility of the M2 when

The replacement for the gun rail on the Half-track Car M2 is the armoured M49 ring mount seen over the driver's compartment. When fitted to the M2 the vehicle became the M2A1. *TACOM*

Visible in this picture of a Half-track Car M2A1 is the canvas bag containing the tripod for the onboard .30-calibre machine gun. Above the stored .50-calibre tripod are the metal hoops for supporting the inclement weather tarp. *TACOM.*

towing a 105mm howitzer, pushed the U.S. Army in September 1941 to design of a larger, heavier, and more powerful model of what was referred to on paper as the Half-track Truck T14.

Plans called for the T14 to weigh approximately 9,090 kg (20,000lb) and to possess both overhead and side armour thick enough to withstand .30-calibre ball ammunition. Called for was an internal payload capacity of 2,550kg (5,600lb), plus the ability to tow a 105mm howitzer. By October 1941, it was clear that the performance parameters desired for the T14 could not work within the weight range specified, resulting in the programme's cancellation before construction of a pilot.

The demise of the T14 did not deter the U.S. Army and work continued on design and development of a suitable armoured half-track truck able to comfortably tow a

105mm howitzer off-road. Therefore, five more half-track trucks were proposed, labelled as the T15, T16, T17, T18, and T19.

The five proposed half-track trucks evolved around the same general specifications. These included an internal payload capacity of 2,730kg (6,000lb), to include a 14-man crew and all-around protection from .30-calibre ball ammunition. Armament was to be a .50-calibre machine gun.

To improve the off-road performance and armour protection of the Half-track M2 there appeared the Half-track Car T16 as pictured. The lengthened vehicle had an enlarged vertical volute spring suspension (VVSS) system and an armoured roof. *TACOM*

In December 1942, it was proposed that a single vehicle, based on the Half-track Personnel Carrier M3, replace both the Half-track Car M2 and the M3. That replacement vehicle seen here received the designation Half-track Car T29. *TACOM*

The U.S. Army considered substituting armoured half-track trucks for Half-track Car M2s as artillery prime movers. Five designs received consideration, but only three were eventually tested, including the Half-track Truck T17 pictured. *TACOM*

The only differences among the five proposed half-track trucks were to be their powertrains and suspension systems. In the end, pilots for only three of the five proposed half-track trucks appeared. Test results from Aberdeen Proving Ground in 1943 proved disappointing, and as the artillery branch had already switched to unarmoured full-tracked prime movers, the Army decided to end the programme.

Originally, the U.S. Army's half-tracks left the factory floor with pneumatic tyres with bullet-sealing inner tubes. Beginning in September 1941, these were replaced by 'combat tyres'. These tyres were specially designed pneumatic tyres made of the highest quality rubber and had many more plies (or layers) than standard commercial pneumatic tyres, which added to the tyre casings' stiffness.

The combat tyres included beadlocks, devices that forced the tyre's beads out against the rims to prevent a deflating tyre from coming off the rim. With beadlocks, the combat tyres mounted onto divided rims, with strengthened sidewalls and shoulders. These tyres could run up to 75 miles deflated depending on the size of the projectile or battlefield fragment that penetrated them.

In June 1941, the U.S. Army authorized the testing of a diesel engine for the M2, and by default its potential use in all other half-track models. The advantages of diesel engines were well known at that time, as they offered improved thermal efficiency, which in turn generated greater range per gallon than their petrol-powered counterparts.

Diesel engines also delivered more torque at low engine speeds than petrol engines, which meant they required fewer gear changes and thus less-complex transmissions. A key human factor in favour of diesel engines for combat vehicles is that their fuel has a far higher flash point—the temperature at which the fuel will ignite—than petrol.

In early 1942, the U.S. Army began to backtrack on its former interest in diesel-engine-powered combat vehicles. An example of this can be seen in a February 1942 memo by General Brehon B. Somervell, Assistant Chief of Staff, calling for a drastic curtailment in the use of diesel-engine-powered vehicles by the U.S. Army's 'Armoured Force', formed in July 1940, the distant predecessor of today's U.S. Army Armor Branch.

Somervell's desire that the armoured force use only petrol-engine-powered combat vehicles became official U.S. Army policy in April 1942, with those diesel-powered vehicles then in the inventory being retained in the United States and used only for training purposes.

Personnel Carrier

A total of 12,391 units of the M3 came off the assembly lines of White, the Autocar Company, and the Diamond T

Motor Company between May 1941 and September 1943. The M3 had no internal ammunition storage compartments as did the M2. It did, however, have a rear door, reflecting its primary purpose as a 12-man infantry squad transport vehicle, although it had seating accommodations for 13 men.

Unlike the M2/M2A1 that had only two side-by-side seats in the very front of the vehicle, the M3/M3A1 had three side-by-side seats in the very front of the vehicle.

The M3 was followed off the production lines by 4,222 units of a slightly modified version designated as the M3A1, between October 1943 and June 1945. The key external identifying feature of the M3A1 configuration, like that of the M2A1, was the added armoured M49 ring mount over the right-hand-side passenger seat and deletion of the centrally located pedestal mount. The added armoured ring mount increased the M3A1's height to 2.7 metres (8 feet 10 inches).

Between May 1944 and June 1945, a total of 2,209 M3s where converted to the M3A1 standard. Another 373 units of various M3 variants no longer needed were also reconfigured into the M3A1 standard between January 1944 and June 1945.

Mortar Carrier

Built in far fewer numbers that than M2/M3 was the 7,890kg (17,350lb) 81mm Mortar Carrier M4. Only 572 units were constructed from August 1941 to October 1942 by White. Based on the M2, the M4 retained the large ammunition storage compartments on either side of the vehicle, located directly behind the front seats. The U.S. Army's 81mm Mortar M1 originated from a French design and went into large-scale production beginning in late 1939.

From a July 1942 U.S. Army armoured force manual titled *81mm Mortar Squad and Platoon* appears this extract: "The mortar, being mounted in a half-track vehicle, has excellent cross-country mobility and under most conditions of terrain can follow tanks and other vehicles without loss of distance. It may be moved rapidly into position and fired either from the vehicle or the ground. It will usually be fired from the carrier."

The manual goes on to describe some of the intended roles the 81mm Mortar Carrier performed in an armoured division: "To support the battalion [tank or armoured infantry] or its components by fire on hostile machine guns, anti-tank guns, mortars, and personnel. To fire on targets defiladed from other weapons. For fire on areas where hostile installations have not been definitely located ... To neutralize the action of hostile anti-tank guns and automatic weapons."

As the mortar on board the M4 was also intended to be fired from the ground, the vehicle was provided a rear door, while still retaining the interior gun ring of the M2. Due to the restricted traverse of the mortar on the M4, it was decided to reconfigure the rear compartment of the vehicle to provide the onboard mortar greater traverse. This resulted in the introduction of the 8,180kg (18,000lb) 81mm Mortar Carrier M4A1.

The 600 units of the M4A1 were completed between May 1943 and October 1943 by White. It can be easily distinguished from the earlier M4 by addition of two large storage boxes fitted to the rear of the passenger compartment. The M4A1 had

Left: There were ten seats in the Half-track Personnel Carrier M3 troop compartment, with three more, side by side, in the driver's compartment. While the Half-track Car M2's two 30-gallon fuel tanks were on either side at the rear of the troop compartment, those on the M3 appear on either side. *Patton Museum*

Below: The Half-track Personnel Carrier M3, with the addition of the M49 ring mount seen over the driver's compartment, received the designation M3A1. Notice the sizeable inclement weather tarp strapped to the vehicle's right front fender. *TACOM*

On the Half-track Personnel Carrier M3A1 pictured we see the vertical canvas bag for storing the tripod for the onboard .50-calibre machine gun. Notice that the stored metal hoops for erecting the inclement weather tarp would come off before opening the rear troop compartment door. *TACOM*

authorized storage for 96 rounds of 81mm mortar ammunition as did the M4.

As time went on, the users in the field indicated that what they wanted was an 81mm mortar that fired over the front of a half-track. The result was the assembly by White of 110 units between January 1944 and March 1944 of a vehicle designated as 81mm Mortar Carrier M21. It weighed 9,090kg (20,000lb). Instead of being based on the M2, it was decided to utilize the chassis of the M3 for the M21. It had authorized storage space for 97 rounds of 81mm mortar ammunition.

Among the three modified versions of the Half-track Scout Car T14 there appeared the 81mm Mortar Carrier M4 seen here. Unlike the Half-track Car M2 on which it was based, it came with a rear door to permit the crew to remove the mortar when needed. *Patton Museum*

The Mortar Carrier M4 retained the Half-track Car M2's gun rail and two 30-gallon fuel tanks on either side of the rear of the troop compartment as seen in this picture. Notice the lack of any traverse for the 81mm mortar. *Patton Museum*

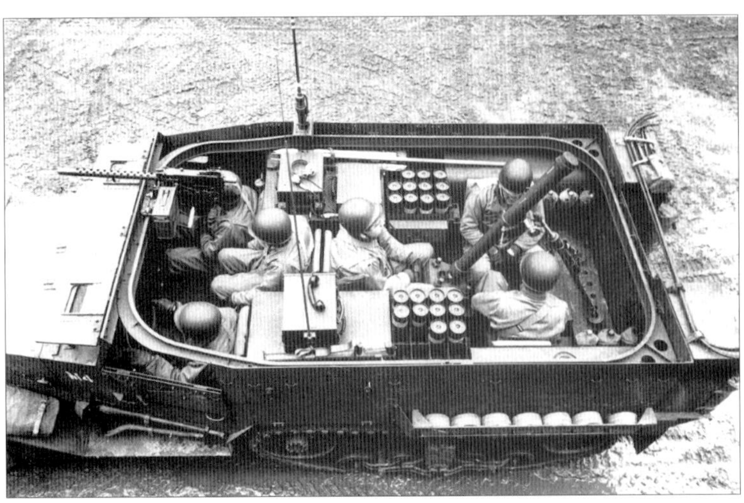

The 81mm Mortar Carrier M4A1 retained most design features of the M4, a significant improvement with the M4A1 proved to be the onboard mortar's increased traverse range. *TACOM*

From the after-action report of the 15th Armoured Infantry Battalion August 1944–May 1945 appears this passage on the employment of their 81mm mortar-equipped half-tracks in April of 1945:

"For the most part of the month, our task was the exploiting of the break-through of the enemy lines. The formation used was one married platoon, assault gun platoon and mortar platoon in the advance guard. The remainder of the Task Force comprised the main body. It was found that by keeping the mortars [81mm] well up in the column, they were able to give quick support when the point ran into resistance and enabled the advance guard to quickly over-run most of the resistance encountered without undue loss of time."

In December 1942, due to a request from the U.S. Army Chemical Warfare Service, developmental work began at Aberdeen Proving Ground on fitting a 4.2mm mortar to fire over the rear of an M4. In spite of installing a two-inch-thick rubber mat under the mortar's base plate, the weapon's recoil caused serious damage to the pilot vehicle's frame.

The next step proved to be mounting the 4.2-inch mortar in a forward-firing position on to the reinforced chassis of an M3A1, relabelled as the T21E1. Test results were promising, but as the U.S. Army now favoured a full-track mortar carrier, the T21E1 programme ended in March 1945.

Tank Destroyers

Reflecting the versatility of the Half-track Personnel Carrier M3 chassis, it was modified to serve in a variety of interim roles, as had been the Half-track Car M2. One of the roles for the M3 proved to be as a tank destroyer, or what the U.S. Army officially labelled as a Gun Motor Carriage (GMC).

In June 1941, a team of U.S. Army Ordnance Department personnel at Aberdeen Proving Ground, Maryland, took a Half-track Personnel Carrier M3 chassis and mounted on it the normally towed 75mm Gun M1897A4 and the upper portion of its wheeled carriage as an experiment. The pilot vehicle received the designation 75mm GMC T12.

The combination of the M1987A4's upper and lower wheeled carriage had its own designation as the M2A3 and came with a small attached gun-shield. The 75mm Gun M1897A4 was an American-built version of the famous 'French 75' that the U.S. Army had used during the First World War.

Such was the desperation of the U.S. Army for whatever mobile firepower it could

(Continues to page 49)

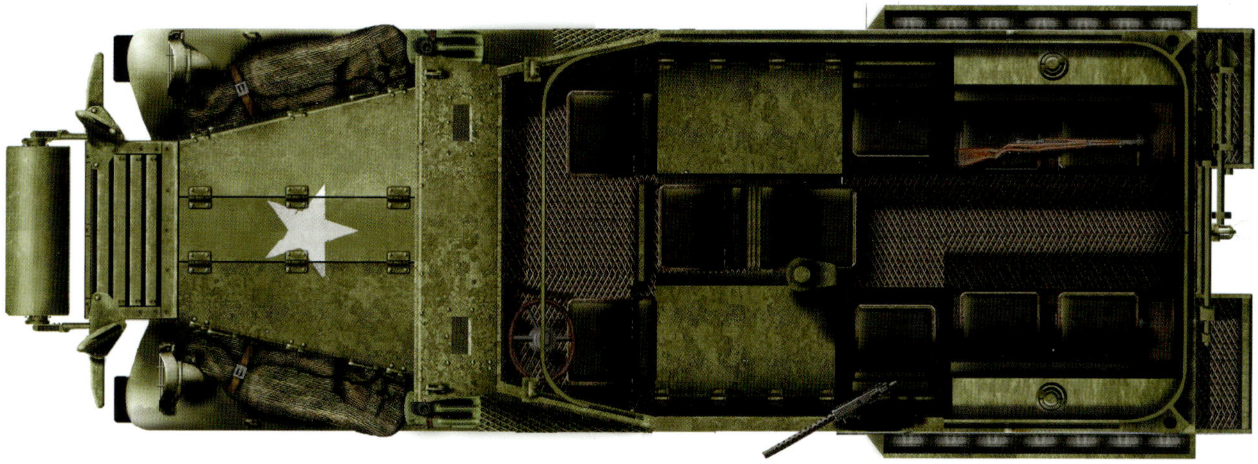

Combat loaded, the 10-man M2 Half-track Car weighed approximately 19,000lbs. Constructed of face-hardened armour it only provided protection against light machine gun fire at certain ranges. The vehicle's armoured windshield had a thickness of 12.7mm and was sloped at 25 degrees.

The 75mm Howitzer Motor Carriage T30 had a crew of five and a combat-loaded weight of approximately 20,000lbs. There was authorized storage onboard the vehicle for sixty rounds of 75mm main gun ammunition. The 75mm howitzer had only 45 degrees of traverse, 22.5 to the left and 22.5 to the right.

The 37mm Anti-tank Gun M3 mounted on an unknown number of Half-track Car M2s by the 2nd Armored Division was strictly an improvised arrangement. The gun and its armoured shield had originally been fitted to a 4x4 light truck designated as the M6 intended only as a training vehicle, but still went to North Africa.

The 75mm Gun Motor Carriage M3, had a five-man crew and due to the weight of the 75mm main gun and its armored shield weighted about 20,000lbs. There was authorized storage on the vehicle for 57 main gun rounds. The listed firing rate for the 75mm main gun was 20 rounds per minute.

With seating for 13 men the Half-track Personnel Carrier M5 had a combat weight of 20,500lbs. An International Harvester Company modified counterpart to the M3s built by the first three commercial contractors it weighed in at 20,500 pounds. Rather than face-hardened armor it had been built of welded homogeneous steel armor.

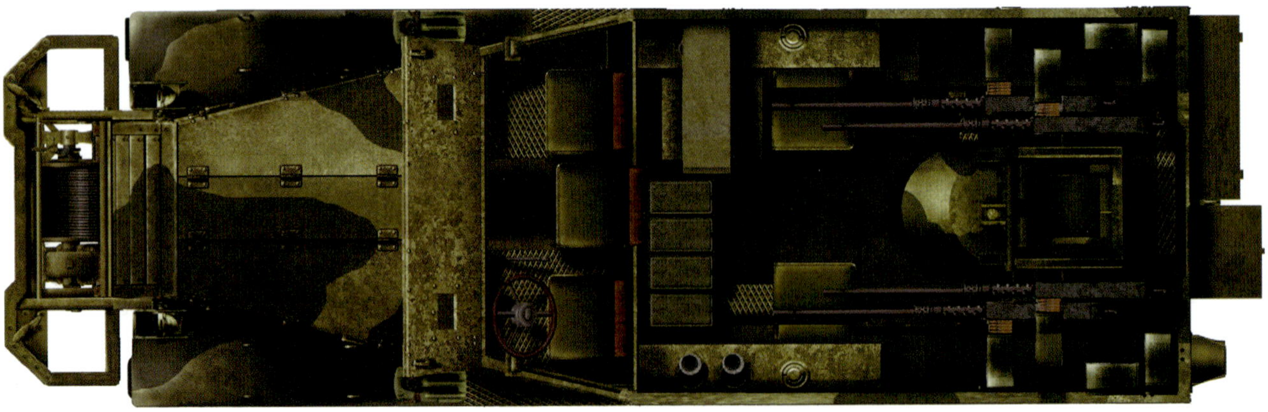

The Multiple Gun Motor Carriage had a crew of five-men and weighted 19,000 pounds. On the vehicle there was authorized storage for 5,000 rounds for the four .50 caliber machine guns. The armored gun mount had 360 degrees of traverse and a traverse rate of 60 degrees per second.

The M21 81mm Motorized Mortar Carrier had a crew of five men. Combat loaded it weighed in at 20,000 pounds. The forward-firing mortar had a manual traverse rate of 11 degrees right and left. Elevation ranged from 60 to 45 degrees. There was onboard storage for 90 rounds of ammunition.

The six-man 105mm Howitzer Motor Carriage T19 weighed combat loaded 20,000 pounds. Traverse of the 105mm howitzer was limited to 20 degrees left and right. Maximum elevation came out to 35 degrees plus. Only 324 examples of the vehicle were built in 1942.

M2

NJARNG 117th Cav 'Essex Troop'

1/35 Scale

Brian Bocchino

This is the Dragon M2/M2A1 2-in-1 half-track built as a M2. The original intention was to build it as a NJARNG 117th Cav 'Essex Troop' vehicle. The unit had an impressive history during the Second World War. However, sufficient reference material, with the unit markings for that vehicle, could not be found, and they have thus been left off the model but may indeed be added in future should the references become available. The two figures are from Dragon and the shrine is from a Verlinden set. The cobble stone road is made from cork and plaster.

View of the M2A1 US Halftrack stopped at a roadside shrine.

Frontal view of the vehicle with the grills in the closed position.

View of the front driver side with some tools visible.

Right side of the vehicle.

Rear view of the vehicle with two soldiers gathered by the shrine.

A look in the crew area with miscellaneous gear spread out.

Left side of vehicle
including the ground work.

M2 IN ITALY

M3A1

23rd Tank Battalion, 12th Armoured Division

1/35 Scale

Brian Richardson

Dragon's 1/35 3-in-1 kit #6332 is a well-moulded kit with no sink marks or flash present and provides optional parts for an M3, M3A1 or M3A2. The kit builds up in a logical sequence starting with a basic engine and moving through the chassis and suspension which are common to all three variants with just a couple of choices to be made between an M3 and M3A1. Dragon's instructions for some of their 3-in-1 kits have come in for criticism as being too confusing but if the modeller takes time deciding on which variant first up and studying the instructions here shouldn't have too much trouble with this one.

In step 18 the front and rear cab sections are brought together and joined to the chassis. I chose to glue the halves of the cab together first to avoid any potential alignment problems later that might have occurred if they were joined to the chassis separately. After this had set I found there is a tight fit between the locating lugs on the front half which were difficult to insert into the slots provided on the chassis rails and after a little trimming everything fitted well.

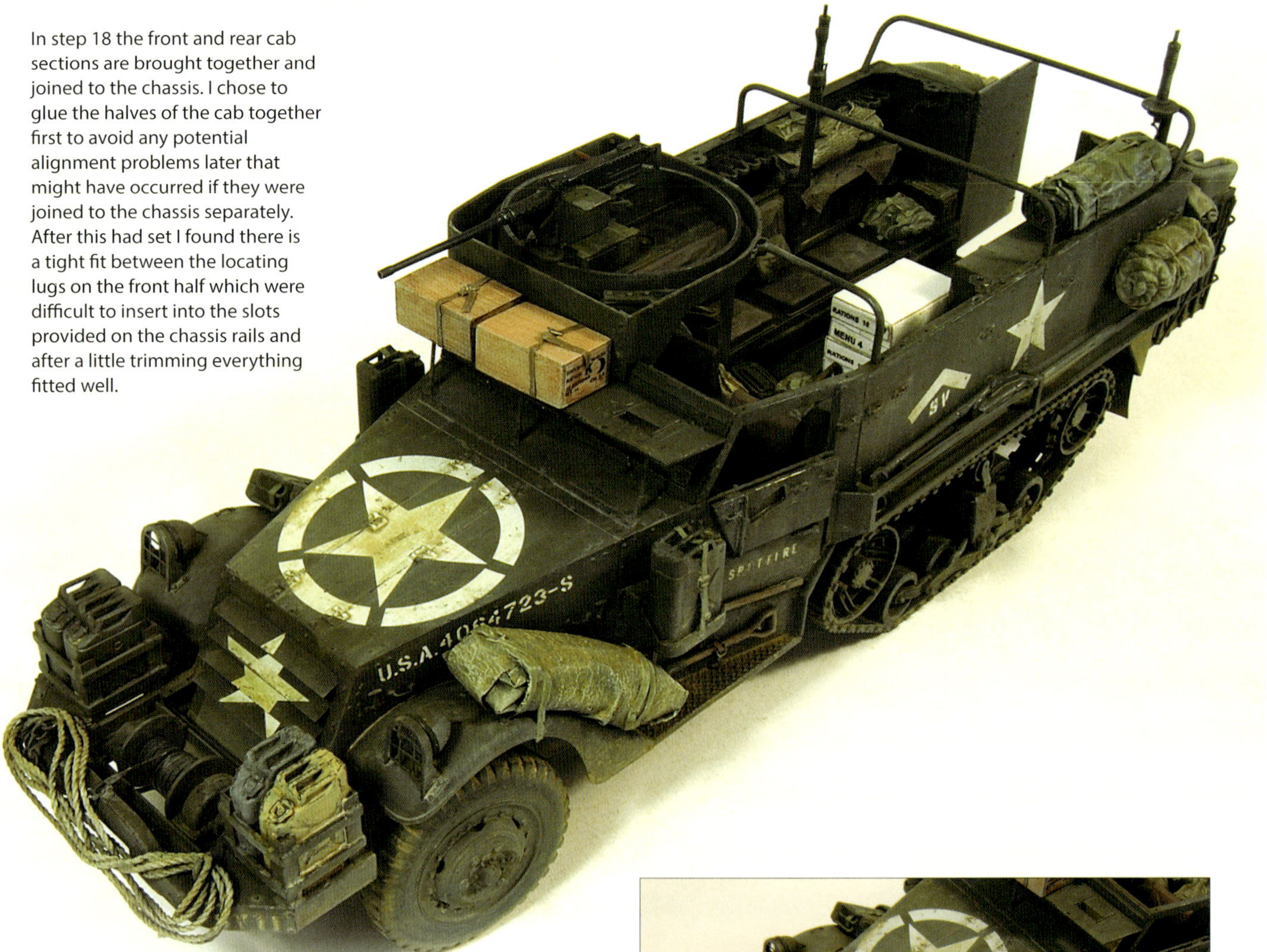

Both jerry can racks have been replaced and Italeri cans substituted with Tamiya tape straps.

Dragon provide five decal options and have included a full sheet of alphabet letters and numbers so the modeller can choose to do any vehicle. They respond very well to decal softener. I was expecting trouble with the bonnet star settling around the hinges and panel lines, but had no silvering whatsoever. I also use a hair dryer to help soften them and pull them down around any raised details.

At step 13 for an M3A1 the side walls F21 and F22 are mated to the lower hull tub F6: these need to be a tight fit to avoid misalignment with the front cab section when they're brought together. The side plates of both front and rear sections should be flush at the join behind the driver's doors.

Many half-tracks had field workshop fabricated storage bins and these were scratched from card, evergreen rod and copper wire. These have been filled with a mix of resin boxes, Milliput tarps, blankets and bedrolls. I've replaced all the tie downs with thin copper wire and added the exhaust support bracket that Dragon missed.

The solid moulded door handles were replaced with resin parts.

Painting the O/D was a mix of Tamiya XF-62 Olive Drab and XF-60 Dark Yellow. This seemed a little dark when the gloss sealing coat went on and I've tried to bring it back with light earth coloured Humbrol enamel washes. I've used a mix of kit decals, leftovers and Verlinden dry transfers to represent a service vehicle of the service company belonging to the 23rd Tank Battalion, 12th Armoured Division.

M4

US Army Western Front, 1944

1/35 Scale

Gary Riley

This is a Dragon models M4 81mm Mortar Carrier kit #6361 representing the U.S. Army in Europe. Ammo by Mig paints was used: the Olive Drab modulation set and it was weathered with Ammo by Mig enamel washes, streaking grime and rain streaks. Vallejo pigments were also used.

PROWLER

PROWLER

PROWLER

PROWLER

PROWLER

M16 MGMC

482nd AAA AW/SP Battalion, Belgium 1944/45

1/16 Scale

Brian Richardson

The 482nd AAA AW/SP Battalion was attached to the 9th Armoured Division from October 1944 until May 1945 and were instrumental in the defence of Bastogne and St Vith, Belgium during the Battle of the Bulge and later defending the Ludendorff Bridge at Remagen, March 1945. Trumpeter's kit is reasonably accurate although it's missing quite a few details, however these can be added with some scratch building.

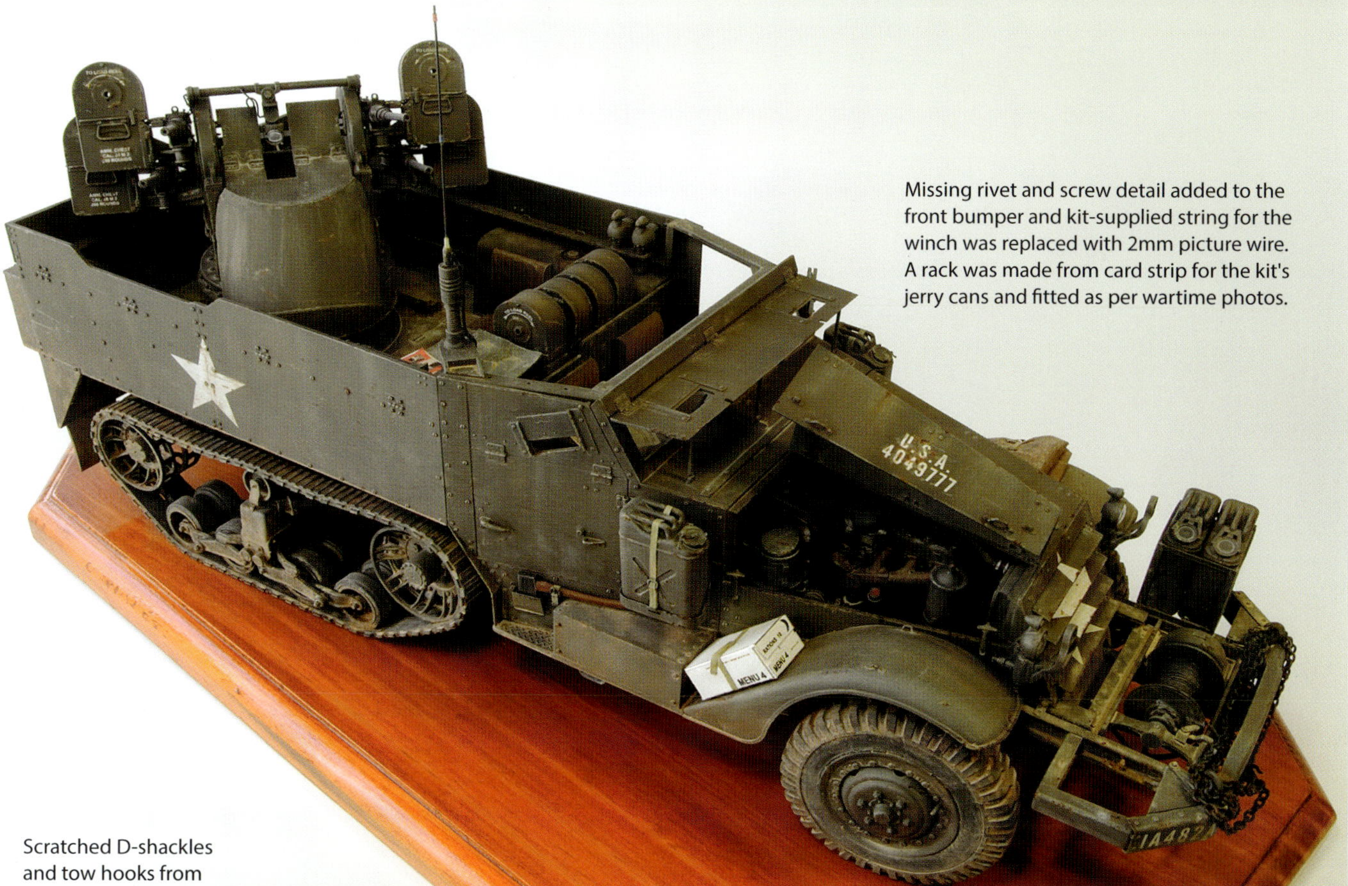

Missing rivet and screw detail added to the front bumper and kit-supplied string for the winch was replaced with 2mm picture wire. A rack was made from card strip for the kit's jerry cans and fitted as per wartime photos.

Scratched D-shackles and tow hooks from copper wire.

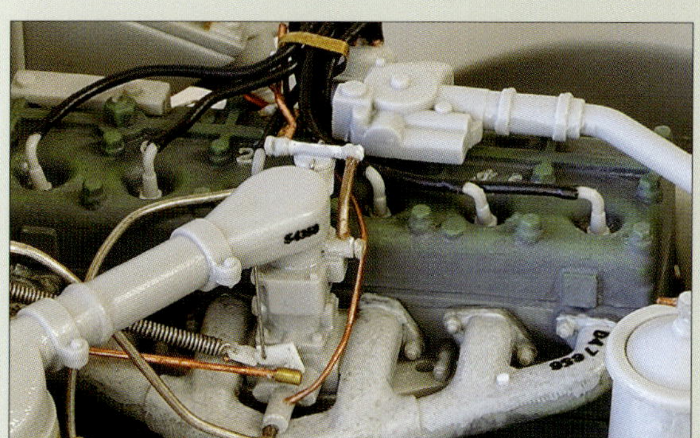

Added shock absorber arms and steering linkage from rod, aluminium strip and detailed with various nuts and bolt heads, brake lines from 0.4mm copper wire and added the missing bump stops to the top of the leaf springs.

Moving to the engine compartment I've added mesh to the radiator, armoured louver screws, pulley drive belts, plug leads, wiring, foundry numbers to the exhaust manifold. The differential and final drive housings are also missing a few bolts.

Kit one-piece vinyl tracks are very stiff and difficult to fit without breaking the road wheel axles so new ones were laminated from different thickness plastic card.

The driver's cab has bolt detail, map pocket, wiper motors, two fire extinguishers added. The driver's door hinged flap was cut and lowered with latch details added. The moulded on door handles were also replaced with new ones carved from styrene.

The muffler assembly was detailed and fitted with its missing support bracket. The rear idler wheel's support arm was made from rod. Missing tie downs made from copper wire have been added to both front mud guards, driver's doors and around the top rail rear compartment.

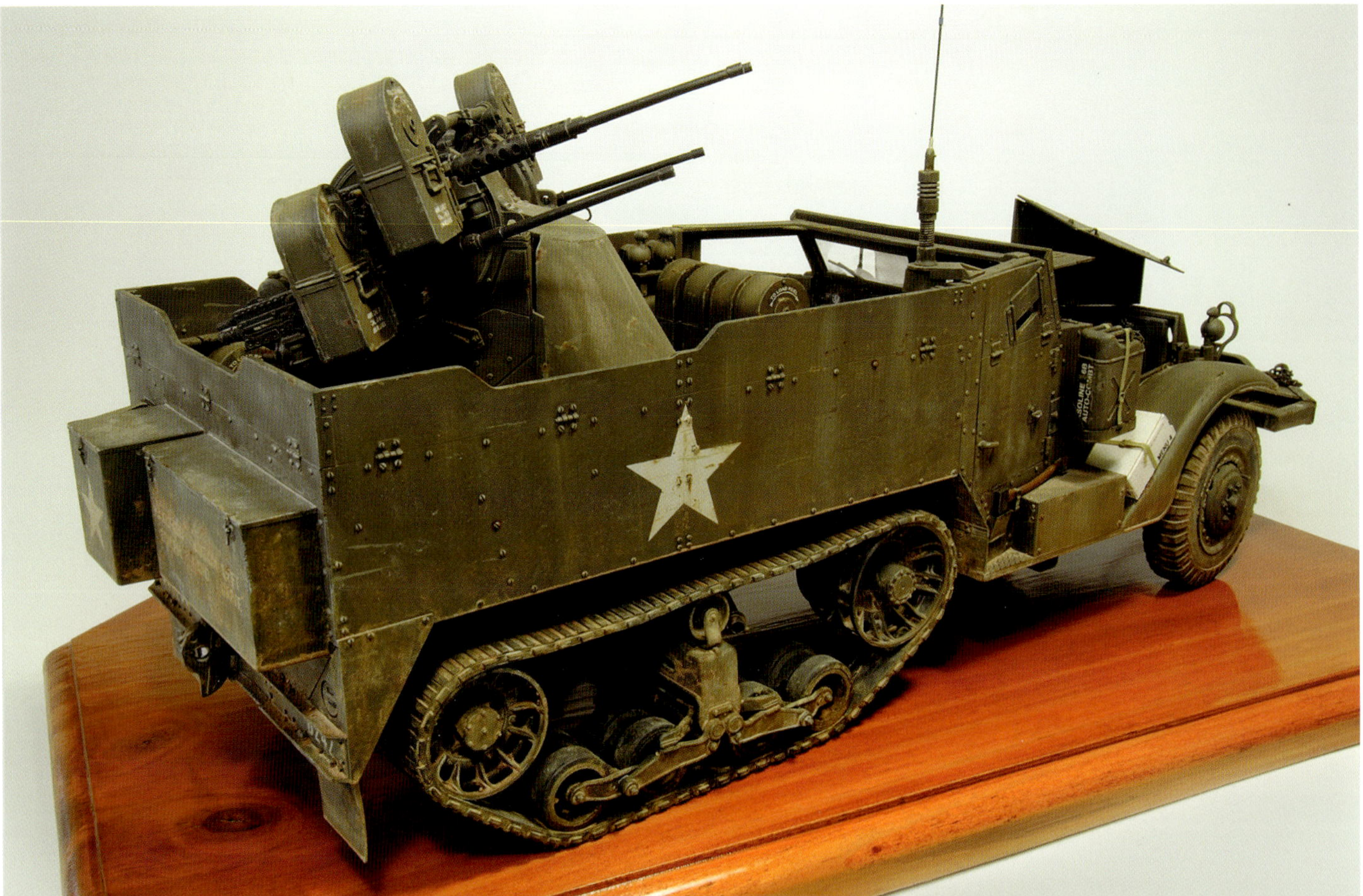

The Maxson turret has had missing welds and bolt detail added plus the Briggs and Stratton engine and battery detailed. There's four spare 0.50cal gun barrels added, one each side of the turntable and two fitted to the drop side.

Dragon released its M2A1 Half-track 2-in-1 kit in 2006. Prior to that the only kit available was produced by Blue Tank Models. The first US Army Half-track Personnel Carrier M3 was released in the 1940s by Mod-Ac and included some wood parts. After that, Monogram, in its various guises, offered the only other half-track kits, until 1972, which were the MGC M3 and Personnel Carrier M3A1 in 1/35 scale. These are now only available second hand and Nitto's 1/72 release is also no longer available. Tamiya stepped onto the scene three years later with an Armoured Personnel Carrier M3A2 Half-track, which is still around. Academy released a M3A2 in the early 1980s and then reboxed it with MiniCraft a few years later. In the late 2000s Academy released a ground vehicle set that includes a Half-track Personnel Carrier M3. Both these kits are available in 1/72 scale. The majority of Academy's range depicts the Bradley, a designation only given to half-tracks in service after the Second World War. Black Dog also has a multi-kit available with a M3 and an amphibious vehicle, in the same vein as the Academy kit minus the Harley Davidson. Fortunately for modellers Dragon took advantage of the scarcity of half-track kits in 2008 and has steadily built its range since then, releasing five kits of half-tracks used in the Second World War. Of the variants, many kits are around and there should be sufficient to satisfy most modellers' needs. Bolt Action has a 1/56 scale M3A1 and a M21 Mortar Carrier in its range and Blitzkrieg Miniatures also have an M3A1 and a M5/M9 available.

ACADEMY

There are quite a few errors in the M3 from Academy's ground set: the rear lights are a bit too far out and a bit too big, the reinforcement bars in the interior stowage bins are missing as are the rifle racks inside them, the central guide rail on the inside of the continuous rubber tracks is missing as is the groove on the outside. Academy gives modellers the choice between open and closed engine louvres at the front of the engine compartment and a choice between a winch and a roller. Ejector marks are strategically located and except on the front hull the fit is good. With some scratch building the model can be downgraded to a M3 and with a little time a decent display piece can be built from this kit.

ITALERI

The Italeri Fast Assembly US M3 Half-Track plastic half-track model is in 1/72 scale. For beginners and war gaming the build can certainly stand-alone but for a display model it requires the use of some aftermarket products; it is an early model M3 half-track without the ring mounted HMG, instead it is on a pintle mount in the passenger compartment with no mine racks on the sides either. Italeri also offers a M3 75mm GMC Half-track.

DRAGON

Dragon's M2/M2A1 2-in-1 kit is in 1/35 scale and comes with five decal options: M2 1st Armoured Division, Italy 1944 or Tunisia 1942; M2 US Army 1941/42; M2A1 XX Corps, Belgium 1945; M2A1 US Army 1941/42 (although this must be a typo as the M2A1 was not produced until 1943). The standard of the moulding is good, with clean crisp parts, with only the usual array of plastic knock out nodes that need removing. The detail on this kit is good, especially on the suspension compartments. However, the screw heads on the side armour plates appear as rivets due to a moulding error. It come with four radiator panels, two rear compartment walls, two styles of head lights, a full skate ring or pedestal mount and other alternative parts. With all this why not then include some 'normal' tyres for those who don't want to modify their kit. The M3 75mm GMC has seven decal options available, including 601 Tank Destroyer Battalion, Tunisia 1943; Sicily 1943; 2nd Marines Saipan 1944; 1st King's Dragoon Guards, 1944 and 1945 as well as A Squadron 27th Lancers, Italy 1945. "The tires, as presented in the 1/35 scale Dragon kits are a major point of contention between scale modellers. Dragon provides them moulded as 'flat', which is incorrect considering the manufacture of U.S. tires during that time period. Although the hood is not cut away to open and if you want to see the beautiful engine detail you need to do this yourself, Dragon's half-track kits are popular, welcome additions. Other Second World War half-track kits include: M3A1, T19 105mm Howitzer Motor Carriage and a M21 Mortar Motor Carriage. Dragon has included a M4 81mm Mortar Carrier in its range for which the Eduard M4 half-track is designed to be assembled with.

This is the Dragon kit (6467) of the M3 75mm Gun Motor Carriage. The unit markings represent the Royal Canadian Dragoons, 1st Canadian Infantry Division, Italy, September 1944. The M3 is painted in the American Olive Drab No. 9 colour using Polly Scale paint #505098, which is their equivalent of US olive drab, and is acrylic. The figures are from Ultracast. The kit was weathered using acrylic and oil washes followed by dusting with pastel chalks. The front tires have been replaced with Hussar as the Dragon tires have an under-inflated look.

The engine compartment was opened for display and some scratch-built parts such as spark plugs, wiring, distributor have been added as the kit engine lacked detail. Also added are Minor photo etch jerrycan mounts.

The decals used are from Quartermaster and the kit set.

Images and model courtesy of Dave Watson.

HASEGAWA

Hasegawa's M3A1 in 1/72 scale has rubber band tracks that lack detail and look a bit basic. The kit comes with five crew members, on which the detail is soft, but a nice anti-slip mesh 'mat' covers the crew compartment floor. An optional plastic canvas roof is included which, when assembled, looks good. This is considered a reasonable kit with enough detail to pass for a decent build. Hasegawa also has a M4A1 with a detailed mortar compartment and five figures.

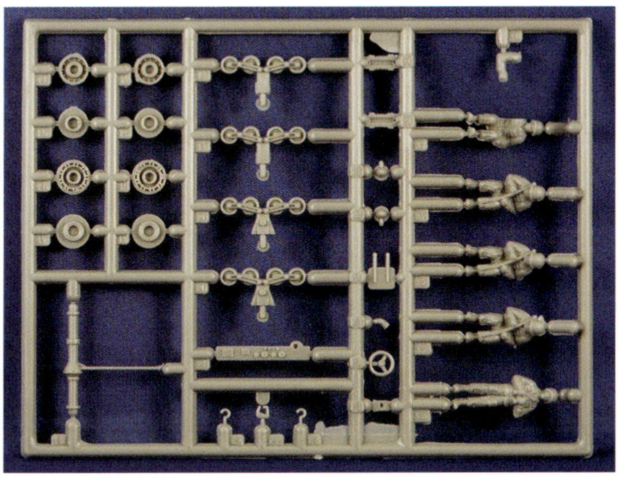

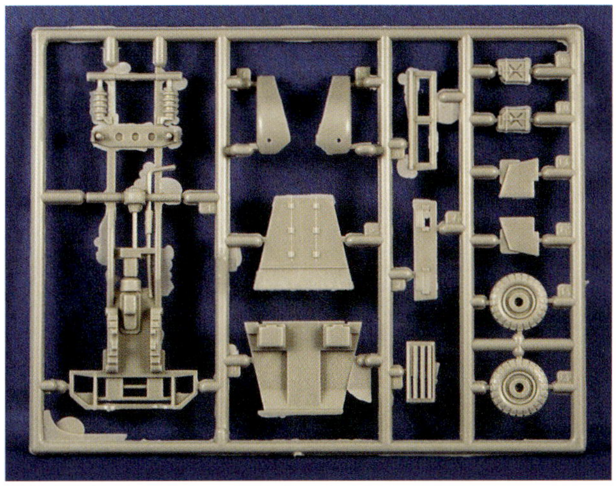

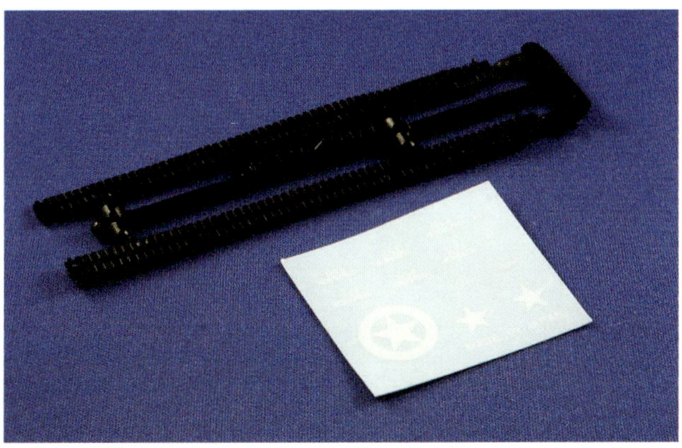

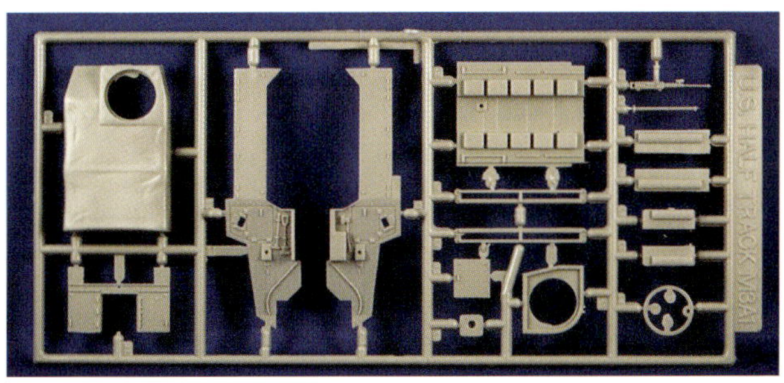

These spruces are from the M3A1 kit. Assemly begins with the chassis which has detail like the driveshaft and exhaust moulded in place. The decal sheet has markings for three unique serial numbers.

MILICAST MODELS

This 1/76 resin cast model manufacturer offers a range of American half-tracks: their M2 and M2A1 kits are available again, as is the M3 and M3A1. Then they offer a M3 75mm half-track GMC, a M4A1 81mm Mortar half-track, a M15 GMC 40mm Bofors SP and a M16 anti-aircraft HT GMC and a T30 75mm HMC. Milicast offer three M14 kits: an ambulance half-track and command half-track both with optional tilt cover and a M14 modified for a personnel role.

Half-track M2.

Half-track M2A1.

Half-track M3 75mm GMC.

Above left and right: Half-track M3.

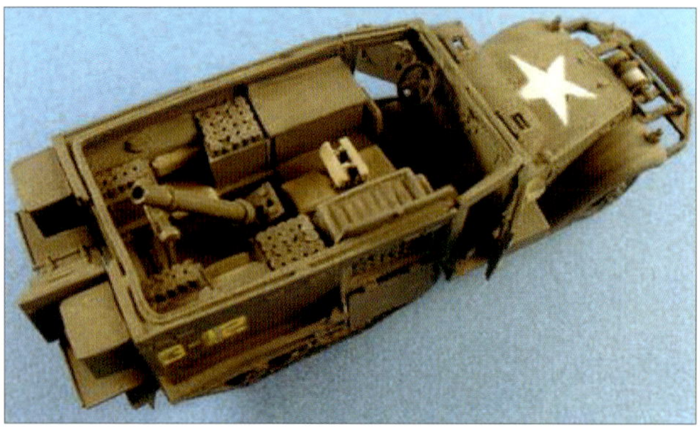

Half-track M4A1.

Tilt Cover for Milicast/Airfix M3/M5 series Halftracks

M15.

M16.

T30.

M14 Command Half-track with optional tilt cover.

Ambulance M14 Half-track with optional tilt cover.

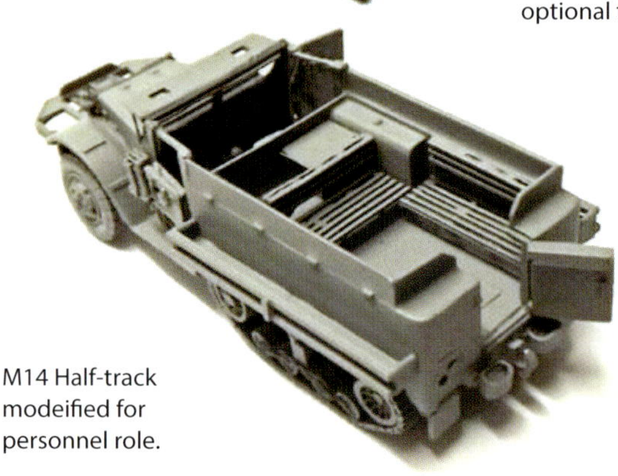

M14 Half-track modeified for personnel role.

PLASTIC SOLDIER

Plastic Soldier's Half-track Personnel Carrier M3 in 1/72 scale includes three vehicles and 24 crew members with options to build either the M3 or M3A1 version with 8 US crew figures per vehicle and extra stowage. As with the M3, their M5 is also a three-vehicle set with enough crew to fill them all. The M5 has many stowage and gun options, the crew members are decent and the kit is easy enough to assemble and has good instructions. It has a completely moulded under carriage, however, there are easier manufacturers' models to assemble. In 15mm (1/100) scale the kit contains five half-track models and 40 crew members.

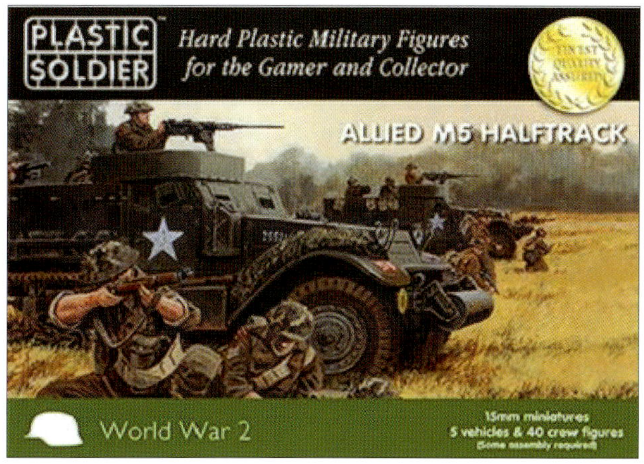

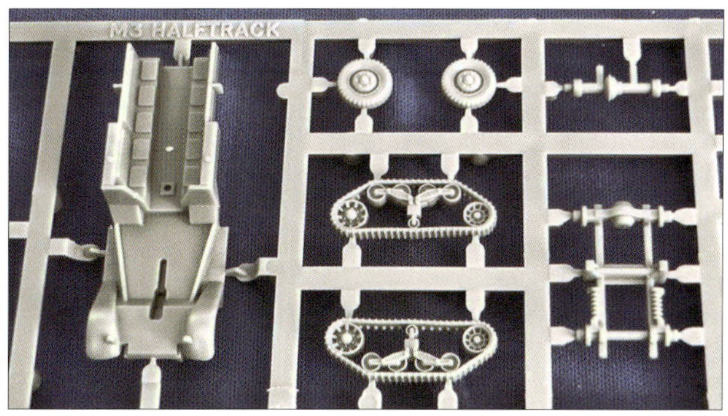

AIRFIX

Known for their ease of assembly, Airfix offers modellers a M3 Half-track & 1 Ton Trailer, except it's not a M3 or a M3A1. When it was released in 1966 an American half-track was just that, variants and subtleties were lost on the teenage market it was aimed at. Now, it comes under heavy scrutiny and is likely a post-war British modified vehicle, possibly a 15cwt cargo carrying conversion. It has numerous accuracy issues, especially in the rear compartment which could be overcome with a tarp. However in its scale of 1/76 it is a very accurate size. One modeller, Nigel Robins, sums the Airfix kit up thus: "... after criticizing the Airfix kit so completely, how do all other models of the M3/M5 series compare? Answer: very poorly. None are better; all kits have their faults. The Fujimi kit is a better-defined carbon copy of the Airfix (perpetuating its faults) though it does give a Maxson turret but is more expensive and is manufactured from hard, nasty Fujimi plastic. The Matchbox kit is under-scale, 2mm too narrow and 1mm too short, feels 'small' elsewhere and the track units are not as nice. In 1/72 the Hasegawa kits are a big 1/72, too wide by 1mm and the cabs are, in my opinion, incorrect, as are the headlights. The Hasegawa kits subsequently look huge compared to the Airfix whilst the Matchbox kit looks tiny."

RUBICON MODELS

Rubicon Models offers a two-sprue base kit in 1/56 scale for the M3 half-track with a choice of building either the M3 or the M3A1. Other options include a Tulsa Model 18G winch, unditching roller, open or closed rear stowage racks with metal boxes, front armoured louvers in open or closed position and various machine gun (both MMG and HMG) choices. A driver and passenger are included. For ease of assembly the kit offers a one-piece engine and truck body. The M21 Mortar Motor Carriage & tarpaulin set is a conversion kit for the M3/M3A1 includes a stand-along mortar team and five infantrymen.

Courtesy www.rubiconmodels.com

TAMIYA

Their US Armoured Personnel Carrier M3A2 Half-track can be backdated to an M3 but the sprockets and idlers are pretty bad, replacement resin ones are available from Verlinden IIRC. The M3A2 is available in two decal options: UA Army 1st Armoured Division and US Army 9th Armoured Division. Blast Models has designed a 10-piece set of stowage and personal equipment. They are resin parts with realistic and well-defined detail and no blemishes to remark upon. The two larger casings unfortunately were designed for the M3A2 non-production version. The nine crew figures include a driver, seven infantry figures in various poses and a walking soldier. A problem with this otherwise quality Tamiya kit is that there are ladders already moulded to the vehicle sides which make placing the decals tricky. Tamiya also has a Half-track 81mm Mortar Carrier M21 with crew and the MGMC M15 available. The screw heads on this kit are correct.

TRUMPETER

Trumpeter's only American half-track is a 1/16 M16 Half-track MGMC plastic model kit. If you want to build something big and eye-catching, this model will fit the bill. It is short on detail though such as with the suspension, driver's compartment and rear compartment interior and the radiator in quite sad but pre-assembled metal hinges for the door and engine are supplied. The armoured panels on the doors and rear compartment are moulded mixed in the upright position. The Maxson mounting and the M2 cal.50s are probably the standout feature of the kit. This is not a kit that can be put together overnight: there is quite a bit of clean up necessary of the mould seams and pin marks but the fit overall is good. Apart from a small decal sheet of instrument dials from Archer dry transfers there's no after market PE or resin updates for this kit so the modeller has to go it alone.

Model by Andrzej Jasiński, with kind permission.

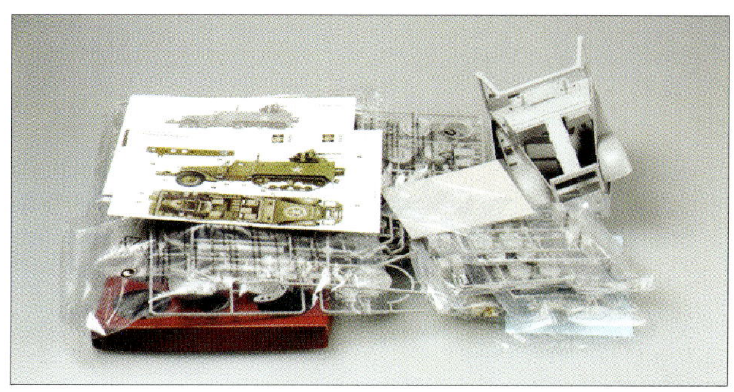

The one-piece hull tubs make assembly much easier and it's multi-media approach with die cast chassis rails, screws, metal hinges and PE are a novel approach. Out of there box it's still an impressive model and with some old fashioned modelling skills can be made into an outstanding build.

Probably the most challenging part of the kit is the tracks, they take time and patience to assemble. Modellers may prefer to break the road wheels off and scratch build new tracks from card.

The kit-supplied wing mirrors are inaccurate. Small round mirrors were mounted to military vehicles not large square/rectangular ones supplied by Trumpeter.

From front to rear quite a bit of plumbing has been added to the engine, Trumpeter completely missed all of this. The missing cross braces in front of the radiator have also been added. In the driver's compartment wiper motors, fire extinguishers and a map pocket with maps has been added. Trumpeter's door handles are moulded solid but on this model have been replaced with separate items.

The cut-outs on the fold-down armor flaps on either side of the M16 (MGMC) allowed the two bottom metal ammunition containers of the Gun Mount M45 to clear the vehicle's rear compartment as it traversed through 360 degrees. The winch placed behind the vehicle's front bumper had a listed 10,000-pound capacity. Power for the winch came from a transmission take-off.

The best part of the kit is the Maxson turret. On the real vehicle's spare 50 cal. barrels were mounted on the floor and side walls. Trumpeter actually supply enough spares to fit them even though their mounts aren't included in the kit.

Model by Andrzej Jasiński, with kind permission.

(Continues from page 16)

field in the summer of 1941 that Autocar was provided the T12 pilot as a template, rather than blueprints, to complete an order for 36 identical copies authorized in July 1941. Some went to the newly formed 93rd Anti-tank Battalion for field testing and others to Aberdeen Proving Ground.

The 75mm Gun M1897A4 firing an armour-piercing capped (APC) projectile at a muzzle velocity of 2,000 feet per second could penetrate 7.5 centimetres (3 inches) of FHA at 900 metres (1,000 yards). A projectile is the part of a round of ammunition that is fired from a weapon by the force of gases produced by the propelling charge contained within a cartridge case.

The term 'capped' refers to a forged steel alloy cap that fits over the normal blunt steel nose of the projectile. The job of the cap is to help relieve the initial stress on impact with armour plate by spreading the energy transfer over a larger area and for a longer period, allowing the mostly undamaged blunt steel nose projectile to penetrate the armour of an enemy tank.

To mount the 75mm Gun M1897A4 and its M2A3 upper carriage into a Half-track Personnel Carrier M3 involved some modifications to the vehicle. External changes included doing away with the two-section shatterproof glass windshield and its supporting frame. With the windshield frame gone, the armoured windshield, with its two direct-vision flaps, was hinged at the bottom, and when in the stored position rested horizontally on top of the rear portion of the bonnet.

Internal changes necessary to convert the Half-track Personnel Carrier M3 into the T12 involved the removal of the vehicle's rear passenger compartment floor, the centrally mounted pedestal mount for the vehicle's machine gun, as well as all the seats and storage compartments for the ten passengers normally transported in that portion of the vehicle. The two 30-gallon fuel tanks on either side of the forward portion of the M3 passenger compartment were relocated to either side of the rear compartment.

With the rear passenger compartment of the Half-track Personnel Carrier M3 stripped, a welded steel box-like base was installed just behind the driver's compartment, upon which sat the 75mm Gun M1897A4 and its M2A3 upper carriage with its gun-shield. This combination of gun, upper carriage, and steel box base received the designation 75mm Gun Mount M3.

The placement of the 75mm Gun M1897A4 and the M2A3 upper carriage in the T12 meant it could only fire over the front bonnet, with a traverse range of just 19° left and 21° right. Gun elevation came out to plus 29° and minus 10°.

A V-shaped notch appeared in the upper centre portion of the T12's armoured windshield, so when in its upright position, there was enough clearance for the barrel of the 75mm Gun M1897A4. The original small vertical gun-shield of the M2A3 upper carriage remained when adapted to fit in the T12.

The T12 had authorized main gun ammunition storage for 59 rounds. Nineteen were stored on horizontal racks within the 75mm Gun Mount M3, which supported

With the onboard inclement weather tarp of the 81mm Mortar Carrier M4A1 installed as pictured, the single external design feature that allows one to distinguish it from its predecessor, the 81mm Mortar Carrier M4, are the two large external metal storage boxes on the rear face of the troop compartment. *TACOM*

Eventually, the U.S. army decided to place the 81mm mortar in the roomier troop compartment of the Half-track Personnel Carrier M3. The result, pictured, received the designation 81mm Mortar Carrier M21. The ladder-like arrangement on the upper portion of the troop compartment was a fold-out storage rack. *TACOM*

Without the 81mm Mortar Carriers M4 and M4A1 gun rail, the 81mm Mortar Carrier M21 had its .50-calibre machine gun mounted on a Pedestal Truck Mount M25 on a raised platform in the rear troop compartment. *TACOM*

The 75mm Gun Motor Carriage (GMC) T12 seen here in August 1941 proved to be the U.S. Army's first expedient tank destroyer. It consisted of the customarily towed 75mm Gun M1897A4 (including its upper carriage and gun-shield), mounted on the modified chassis of the Half-track Personnel Carrier M3. *TACOM*

To provide the gun crew of the 75mm Gun Motor Carriage (GMC) T12 an increased level of protection than that provided by the small vertical gun-shield that came with the 75mm Gun M1897A4, a small number of experimental gun-shields appeared, as pictured. *TACOM*

In this picture, we see the breech end of the M1897A4 gun mounted on the pilot 75mm Gun Motor Carriage (GMC) T12. Also visible is the steel platform created to replace the lower carriage of the customarily towed weapon as well as the ammunition ready rack. *TACOM*

the 75mm Gun M1897A4 and its upper carriage. There were another four enclosed steel boxes on a new sub-floor, each of which had storage space for ten rounds.

For anti-aircraft protection, the T12 received a new pedestal mount for a .50-calibre vehicular machine gun installed in the rear of the gun crew compartment. A single enclosed steel box installed on the new sub-floor contained .50-calibre ammunition.

Testing of the T12 in the field and at Aberdeen Proving Ground led to some changes. The crew initially stood at four men: driver, assistant-driver who also acted as the radioman, gunner, and loader. Due to input from the Armoured Centre, it went to five men with the addition of a gun commander. Feedback from the field also led to the removal of the .50-calibre vehicular machine gun and its pedestal mount.

Due to concerns regarding the limited protection afforded the T12's gun crew by the small vertical gun-shield of the M2A3 upper carriage the U.S. Army sought a new gun-shield design. That eventually resulted in a much larger version that appeared in 1942, which was welded onto the vehicle and provided the gun crew with protection from both the sides and overhead.

Based on what were considered successful trials with the first 36 units of the T12, the order increased in July 1941 to a total of 86 units. These were constructed between August 1941 and September 1941 and retained the T12 designation.

In October 1941, the U.S. Army standardized the T12 as the 75mm GMC M3 and placed an order for 2,116 units, with production beginning in February 1942. Due to a shortage of M2A3 gun mounts, some of the last of the GMC M3s built used parts from an older model gun carriage labelled the M2A2.

Fearing Japanese military intentions in the Pacific, beginning in late 1941 the U.S. Army shipped to the Philippines, 50 units of the T12. These were intended to bolster U.S. Army units tasked with the defence of the Philippine island of Luzon. However, with the overwhelming Japanese force arrayed against them in December 1941, eventual defeat was a foregone conclusion, and American troops in the Philippines finally surrendered in April 1942.

A small number of the T12s survived the fighting and were placed in service by the Imperial Japanese Army to aid in repelling the U.S. Army's return to the Philippines. They did not last long when up against the now well-equipped U.S. Army during its return in 1944.

With America's official entry into the Second World War in December 1941, the original plans of the United States Marine Corps (U.S.M.C.) senior leadership called for two tank destroyer battalions assigned at the corps level. This arrangement was never put to the test, as the sole U.S.M.C. tank destroyer battalion organized in

September 1942 found itself disbanded in December 1943 before ever seeing action.

The U.S.M.C. originally ordered 60 units of the 75mm GMC M3 from the U.S. Army in January 1942, but it turned out only 30 were then available. The order for another 219 units was placed in the fall of 1942, due to the U.S. Army's cancellation of the 75mm GMC M3A1, which the U.S.M.C. had intended to order as the replacement for the 75mm GMC M3. The full-tracked 3-inch Gun Motor Carriage (GMC) M10, based on the M4A2 medium tank chassis, was regarded by the U.S.M.C. as too heavy for amphibious operations.

In the end, only the special troop echelon of each U.S.M.C. division received a single battery of 12 units of the 75mm GMC M3. These, in turn, were subdivided with each of the division's three infantry regiments assigned a platoon of four 75mm GMC M3s. Each U.S.M.C. infantry division also had two 75mm GMC M3s in an anti-tank company.

In July 1942, the combination of the 75mm Gun M1897, and modified part of the M2A2 upper carriage, and the steel box mount they sat on received the label 75mm Gun Mount M5. Those vehicles fitted with the 75mm Gun Mount M5 became the 75mm GMC M3A1.

Due to an anticipated shortage of M1987A4 guns for mounting on the 75mm GMC M3/M3A1, in March 1943 the U.S. Army authorized a modified version of the 75mm Gun M3, as fitted in the Medium Tank M4 Series, to be mounted in the 75mm GMC M3. With this new gun, the vehicle received the designation 75mm GMC T73. By the time testing of the T73 was completed the requirement for additional half-track-based tank destroyers had vanished and the programme ended.

The introduction of the M10, production of which began in September 1942, resulted in the construction of the 75mm GMC M3/M3A1 coming to an end in April 1943, with 842 units completed. The other 1,360 units of the Half-track Personnel Carrier M3 chassis allocated for conversion to tank destroyers were converted into the personnel carrier configuration.

A total of 170 units of the 75mm GMC M3 went to the British Army under Lend-Lease. These were primarily assigned to their armoured car regiments and remained in service from North Africa through the Italian campaign, with a few showing up in France in the summer of 1944.

The successful conversion of the Half-track Personnel Carrier M3 into the 75mm GMC M3 led to the decision in March 1942 to develop what became the 57mm GMC T48. It consisted of the 57mm Gun M1 fitted into a Half-track Personnel Carrier M3 chassis.

To support the weight of the 57mm anti-tank gun (when in transit) a travel lock went onto the vehicle's bonnet. As with the 75mm GMC M3, a V-shaped notch had to be cut into the armoured windshield of the T48, when in the raised position, to clear the gun barrel.

The arrangement of the 57mm anti-tank gun in the T48 mirrored that of the M1897 gun in the 75mm GMC M3. It included a specially designed gun shield that provided a degree of side and overhead protection for the gun crew. The gun itself and upper carriage sat on a steel mount designated as the 57mm gun mount T5. Traverse of the gun was limited to 27.5° left and 27.5° right. The maximum elevation came out to plus 15° and minus 5°.

From the U.S. Army Ordnance Catalogue of 1944/1945 is this passage describing the performance of the 57mm anti-tank gun on the GMC T48: "Using AP [armour-piercing] projectile, M70, with a muzzle velocity of 2,800 feet per second, it will penetrate 2.2 inches of face-hardened armour plate at 1,000 yards ... A pivoted gunner's seat is provided, and swings independently of the gun."

A total of 962 units of the T48 were constructed between December 1942 and May 1943 by Diamond T. The original plan called for the bulk to go under Lend-Lease to the British Army, per their request. However, the British Army later decided it had no requirement for the vehicle and took delivery of only 30 units, which in turn went off to

In October 1941, an upgraded version of the 75mm Gun Motor Carriage (GMC) T12 received the designation 75mm Gun Motor Carriage (GMC) M3, with an example pictured. Making room for the 75mm gun required relocating the two 30-gallon fuel tanks to either side of the rear of the troop compartment. *TACOM*

In the mould of the 75mm Gun Motor Carriage (GMC) M3, the Ordnance Department came up with the pilot vehicle pictured referred to as the 57mm Half-track Gun Motor Carriage (GMC) T48. Armed with the M1, an American modified copy of a British 57mm anti-tank gun, and protected by a newly designed gun-shield, it went only to Lend-Lease recipients. *TACOM*

This photograph taken in November 1941 shows the final gun-shield design for the 75mm Gun Motor Carriage (GMC) T12. It raised the vehicle's height to 2.5 metres (8 feet 2 inches). The gunner relied on the Telescope M33 to acquire targets and aim the gun. *TACOM*

With success in employing the modified chassis of the Half-track Personnel Carrier M3 as an expedient tank destroyer, it didn't take long for the U.S. Army to consider its employment for a stop-gap self-propelled artillery piece. The result was the pilot of the 75mm Howitzer Motor Carriage (HMC) T30 seen here. *TACOM*

the Indian Army, the only Commonwealth Army to have been supplied the vehicle.

The decision then came about to provide 650 units of the T48 to the Red Army under Lend-Lease. In Red Army service they received the designation SU-57. A single example of the T48 would be retained by the U.S. Army, with 281 remaining units ordered converted into the Half-track Personnel Carrier M3A1.

Self-Propelled Howitzers

Despite the continued pre-war encouragement by the Ordnance Department that the artillery branch of the U.S. Army should be looking at the development of self-propelled artillery pieces, both guns and howitzers, nothing happened until the U.S. Army Armoured Force issued a requirement for an assault gun intended to equip both its tank and armoured reconnaissance formations in October 1941.

Artillery pieces classified as guns tend to have long barrels, high muzzle velocities, and flat trajectories below 45° and employed for long-range, indirect fire. Howitzers are typically a short-barrelled weapon with medium muzzle velocity. They are normally fired at relatively steep elevations so the rounds can reach targets hidden from flat-trajectory guns. Variations in the propelling charge change a round's trajectory and range.

As an expedient measure, until such time as a suitable full-tracked self-propelled artillery piece entered service, the Armoured Force asked that a normally towed 75mm Field Howitzer M1A1 go on the chassis of the Half-track Personnel Carrier M3, with a new gun-shield. That request resulted in the construction of two pilot vehicles designated as the 75mm Howitzer Motor Carriage (HMC) T30. A 30-gallon petrol tank sat on either side of the rear compartment.

Testing of the T30 pilots went well enough that production was authorized and began in February 1942 and continued until April 1942, with a total of 312 units completed. In August of that same year, the order came down to convert 108 of the existing T30s into the Half-track Personnel Carrier M3. In November 1942, an additional 188 units of the T30 came off the assembly lines for a total of 500 units.

The T30 showed up in North Africa in November 1942 during Operation Torch with the 1st and 2nd armoured divisions. The March 1942 armoured division TO&E called for a total of 42 units of the T30. The division's armoured reconnaissance company had nine, while each of the division's two armoured (tank) regiments had twelve. The single armoured infantry regiment of the armoured division had nine.

Besides serving in armoured divisions, the T30 also appeared in the cannon companies of infantry divisions serving in North Africa, with six authorized.

Employing both direct and indirect fire, the T30 proved extremely popular during its time in North Africa with the U.S. Army.

The replacement for the T30 would be the full-tracked 75mm HMC M8 that first began appearing in service in November 1942. By 1944, the transition from the T30 to the HMC M8 was complete.

In the same time frame as the T30, there came about a pressing Armoured Force requirement for a self-propelled 105mm howitzer. As it would take time to field the preferred full-track version, the Half-track Personnel Carrier M3 once again became the platform of choice. A pilot received authorization in October 1941 designated as the 105mm HMC T19. As expected, the weight of the forward-firing 105mm Howitzer M2 exceeded the vehicle's load-carrying capacity and led to frame strengthening.

Testing of the T19 proved successful enough that production received authorization in March 1942, with the production of 324 units completed by April 1942. Like the T30, the T19 arrived in North Africa during Operation Torch. It served in both the armoured artillery battalions of armoured divisions and the cannon companies of infantry divisions, to supplement the firepower of the T30 in both the direct and indirect fire modes.

Gun crew protection for the T19 came from a small gun-shield that provided protection only from the front. The replacement for the T19 in armoured divisions proved to be the full-track 105mm HMC M7, which began coming off the production lines in April 1942. In infantry divisions the T19 found itself replaced by the towed 105mm M2 howitzers. Maximum range on the M2 came in at 11,150 metres (12,200 yards).

As with the T30, the T19 would linger in U.S. Army service in ever-smaller numbers until approximately 1944. In July 1945, the vehicle was declared obsolete, resulting in 90 units converted into the Half-track Personnel Carrier M3A1.

At one point there were plans in the works to mount the 105mm Howitzer M3 on the same strengthened Half-track Personnel Carrier M3 as the T19. The vehicle received the designation T38 but no pilot appeared and the project officially ended in May 1943. The 105mm Howitzer M3 consisted of a shortened and lighter version of the 105mm Howitzer M2, with a maximum range of 7,580 metres (8,295 yards).

A modified chassis of a Half-track Personnel Carrier M3 fitted with a 105mm howitzer, was conceived a month before that of a 75mm-howitzer-equipped version, but was rejected. However, the success of the 75mm Howitzer Motor Carriage HMC T30 led to construction of the pilot 105mm Howitzer Motor Carriage (HMC) T19 pictured. *TACOM*

Anti-aircraft Half-tracks

As early as the 1920s some in the U.S. Army realized that aircraft could pose a serious threat to ground forces. Despite three successive interwar U.S. Army coast artillery chiefs recommending that anti-aircraft guns be permanently attached to infantry divisions, nothing happened. The reason was the lack of funding between the world wars for the U.S. Army.

The successful employment of ground attack aircraft by the Luftwaffe during the invasions of Poland in September 1939 and France in the summer of 1940 made a powerful impression on the U.S. Army. The anticipation of having to deal with that aerial threat on future battlefields led the U.S. Army Ordnance Department to set about developing suitable anti-aircraft vehicles for the protection of the U.S. Army's two newly formed armoured divisions, activated in July 1940.

Initial work began in October 1940 and revolved around electrically powered twin-machine-gun turrets on trucks. The trucks lacked the load-carrying capacity or stability needed for the mounting and firing of the machine-gun-armed turrets. A prototype of what later became the Half-track Car M2, therefore, found its way into the programme. Modified, it had a twin-machine-gun electrically powered turret by the Bendix Aviation Corporation installed and received the designation Multiple Gun Motor Carriage (MGMC) T1E1.

Testing of the Bendix twin-machine-gun armed turret in the summer of 1941 uncovered some design issues that resulted in its return to the builder. Fortunately, there arrived on the scene at about the same time another twin-machine-gun electrically powered turret. This example came from the W. L. Maxson Corporation and proved very reliable, leading to the cancellation of the T1E1 with the Bendix turret.

The first successful electrically powered machine-gun turret mounted on the Half-track Personnel Carrier M3, proved to be the Twin .50 Calibre Machine Gun Mount M33 pictured. This particular example lacks its customarily affixed front armoured shield for the gunner. *TACOM*

In early 1942, a modified Half-track Car M2 fitted with the Maxson turret received the designation T1E2. Testing of the Maxson turret on the T1E2 led to its standardization in March 1942 as the Twin .50 Calibre Machine Gun Mount M33. Ammunition for the machine guns of the M33 came in large metal containers, each holding 200 linked rounds. When attached to the machine guns, the linked rounds exited the metal containers via a slot directly into the breech of the weapons.

After experimenting with fitting the M33 on several different types of trucks, a decision came about that the chassis of the Half-track Personnel Carrier M3 would make the best choice. This led to a pilot vehicle designated as the Multiple Gun Motor Carriage (MGMC) T1E4. Following some design changes, the vehicle became the MGMC M13, with the pilot arriving at Aberdeen Proving Ground in December 1942. The vehicle had two 30-gallon gas tanks on either side of the rear compartment.

Right: By mounting the Twin .50 Calibre Machine Gun Mount M33 onto a modified version of a Half-track Personnel Carrier M3, you have the vehicle pictured. It received the designation Multiple Gun Motor Carriage (MGMC) M13 and lacked the rear door of the M3. *TACOM*

Below: The Twin .50 calibre Machine Gun Mount M33 also went onto the modified chassis of the Half-track Personnel Carrier M5 as shown. This combination received the designation Multiple Gun Motor Carriage M14 (MGMC). Like the M13 it lacked a rear door. *TACOM*

Following in the development path of the Multiple Gun Motor Carriage (MGMC) M13 there eventually appeared the Multiple Gun Motor Carriage (MGMC) M16 pictured. It came with a four-gun version of the Twin .50 Calibre Machine Gun Mount M33 designated as the M45. *Michael Green*

To facilitate the ability of the two-gun M33 to fire at minus 10 degrees, the upper portions of the armour on the rear and sides of the M13 hinged downward. Over the front of the vehicle, the two-gun M33 could only be lowered to an elevation of 30 degrees plus. The M13 did not have a rear door as the standard Half-track Personnel Carrier M3, rather, the vertical rear face of the vehicle had two large storage boxes affixed.

With the test results of the M13 meeting all expectations, a production order received approval. A total of 1,103 units came off the assembly lines of White between January 1943 and May 1943. All were intended for use by the U.S. Army. Three battalions equipped with the M13 served with the U.S. Army in Italy.

For Lend-Lease purposes, the M33 went onto a modified Half-track Personnel Carrier M5 chassis. In this configuration, the vehicle received the designation MGMC M14. A total of 1,605 units rolled off the IHC assembly lines between December 1942 and December 1943, with all going to the British Army. As an anti-aircraft vehicle, it proved surplus to their needs. The British Army converted them into personnel carriers.

In spite of the standardization of the twin machine gun armed M13 for U.S. Army service, the Ordnance Department continued with its work on the development of a more effective half-track based anti-aircraft vehicle. If two machine guns were effective, it soon came to pass that four machine guns would be even better. So, in April 1942, development of a modified M33 turret armed with four .50 calibre machine gun received authorization.

A modified four-gun M33 turret arrived at Aberdeen Proving Ground in August 1942, and for experimental purposes went onto a Half-track Car M2. If successful, the four-gun M33 arrangement would go onto the modified chassis of the Half-track Personnel Carrier M3.

The test results of the four-gun M33 were positive and in December 1942, it became the .50 Calibre Machine Gun Mount M45. At the same time, the combination of the M45 fitted onto a Half-track Personnel Carrier M3 chassis was designated MGMC M16.

The M16 lacked a rear door as did the M13. In its place there appeared two large storage boxes affixed to the outside of the rear armour vertical plate. The flaps on the rear and sides of the M16 hinged downward when required. Unlike the hinged armour flaps on the M13, those on the M16 had cut-outs. This became necessary as the two bottom ammunition containers of the four-gun M45 would not clear the armoured flaps when in the upright position as the gun mount traversed through 360-degrees.

In early 1943, the assembled pilot of the M16 went through a final round of modifications at Aberdeen Proving Ground, one of which involved installing a 15-centimetre (6-inch) adaptor between the bottom of the M45 and the floor of the half-track. This modification provided more clearance for the M45 when fired.

To allow for faster reloading of the 200-round .50-calibre metal ammunition containers by the crewmen of the M16 a small two-man horizontal platform began to appear on the rear of the M45 starting with production in late 1944. This addition resulted in the M45 becoming the M45D.

Having passed all the required tests and considered ready for field use, the M16 entered into production. A total of 2,877 units rolled off the assembly lines of White between May 1943 and March 1944. Also, 628 units of the earlier two-gun M13 were converted into the M16 configuration.

Another 109 units of a cancelled half-tracked-based anti-aircraft vehicle labelled as the Twin 20mm MGMC T10E1 also found themselves reconfigured as the M16. The combined total of new-built M16s and converted units came to 3,614 vehicles. For Lend-Lease purposes, the four-gun M45 also went onto a modified version of Half-track Personnel Carrier M5 and received the designation MGMC M17. Production commenced in December 1943 and continued until March 1944 with 1,000 units completed; all were supplied to the Red Army, who in turn passed some to the Polish People's Army.

In the months before Operation Overlord, the planned invasion of France in the summer of 1944, the senior Ordnance Department officer of the U.S. First Army decided that there were not enough M16s on hand. What was available was a large number of towed, four-wheel trailers, designated as the Multiple Cal. 50 Multiple Machine Gun Carriage M51. They featured the same .50 Calibre Machine Gun Mount M45 fitted to the M16. Also, on hand was a surplus of Half-track Cars M2s.

As an expedient measure, the senior First Army Ordnance officer had the four-gun M45s removed from their trailers and mounted on the surplus Half-track Cars M2s. The resulting vehicles received the unofficial designation as the M16B, with First Army documents showing that 332 such conversions took place, which equipped eight battalions. Another unofficial designation for the M16B proved to be M2-45, with the unofficial nickname 'Wasp'.As the M2 did not have the folding rear compartment sides of the M13 or the M16, the four-gun M45 went onto an in-house constructed pedestal tall enough to have it clear the sides and rear of the vehicle when firing below the level of the horizon. Supposedly, other U.S. Army units also made the same conversion employing both the M2 as well as the M3 half-tracks.

Combination Anti-aircraft Gun Half-tracks

In mid-1941, the Coast Artillery Branch of the U.S. Army became interested in the concept of an anti-aircraft vehicle based on the Half-track Car M2. In turn there appeared an official request by the Coast Artillery Branch to the Ordnance Department to pursue such a vehicle concept. The result proved to be four experimental vehicles built in September 1941, with all shipped to Aberdeen Proving Ground in October 1941.

The four experimental half-track anti-aircraft vehicles that arrived at Aberdeen Proving Ground received the designation T28. Armament consisted of an unarmoured mount armed with a single 37mm automatic cannon, which had only entered into production the year before, and twin water-cooled .50-calibre M2 machine guns.

The addition of the lower metal ammunition cans on the quad .50 Calibre Machine Gun Mount M45 fitted to the Multiple Gun Motor Carriage (MGMC) M16, required cut-outs in these folding-down panels for clearance as is visible in this photograph of an M16. *Christopher Vallier*

With the addition of a small metal platform on the rear of the quad .50 Calibre Machine Gun Mount M45 (seen here) for the two loaders (referred to as cannoneers), it received the designation M45D. The metal ammunition containers officially referred to as the M2 Ammunition Chest each held 200 rounds. *Pierre Olivier Buan*

The pilot Half-track Multiple Gun Motor Carriage (MGMC) T28 seen here has as armament a single 37mm automatic cannon and two .50 calibre water-cooled machine guns. The chassis was that of the Half-track Car M2. It did not go into production. *TACOM*

When a requirement arose for a vehicle that had the right armament arrangement to engage both armoured vehicles as well as aircraft, a slightly modified version of the cancelled Half-track Multiple Gun Motor Carriage (MGMC) T28 appeared as pictured. It received the designation T28E1 and found itself rushed into production. *TACOM*

Next in line after the successful combat debut of the Half-track Multiple Gun Motor Carriage T28E1 in North Africa is the vehicle pictured, designated as the Multiple Gun Motor Carriage (MGMC) M15. Instead of two water-cooled .50-calibre machine guns as seen on the T28E1, the M15 had two air-cooled .50-calibre machine guns. *TACOM*

This combination gun mount received the designation M42.

A key advantage of fielding a 37mm anti-aircraft gun was the size of the projectiles it fired. Due to their greater mass, they could destroy a target that machine-gun bullets might strike without seriously damaging it.

Unlike the projectiles fired from larger anti-aircraft guns, equipped with time fuses, mid-range anti-aircraft guns like the 37mm fired a projectile with a super-sensitive fuse that exploded on contact with any portion of an aircraft. A self-destruct mechanism detonated the projectile if it missed its target and began to fall back to earth.

The high-explosive (HE) projectile fired from the 37mm Anti-aircraft Gun M1A2 weighed approximately one pound and left the weapon with a muzzle velocity of 2,600 feet per second. Maximum vertical range was about 5,700 metres (6,200 yards) and horizontal range 8,100 metres (8,875 yards).

Testing of the T28 led the Ordnance Department to recommend to the Coast Artillery Branch that a modified Half-track Personnel Carrier M3 chassis made more sense as a platform than the smaller M2. The Coast Artillery Branch disagreed, and the T28 programme came to an end.

There appeared a recommendation in a June 1941 memorandum from the U.S. Army Services of Supply for the acquisition of 80 units of a 37mm-automatic-cannon-armed vehicle capable of engaging both ground and aerial targets. To the Ordnance Department, the request for a new dual-purpose weapon platform looked like a role suited to the recently cancelled T28.

In July 1941, authorization for 80 units of the Half-track Personnel Carrier M3 chassis fitted with the M42 combination gun mount from the T28 appeared. The vehicle received the designation MGMC T28E1 and came off the Autocar production lines between July 1942 and August 1942.

When a requirement arose for a vehicle that had the right armament arrangement to engage both armoured vehicles as well as aircraft, a slightly modified version of the cancelled Half-track Multiple Gun Motor Carriage (MGMC) T28 appeared as pictured. It received the designation T28E1 and found itself rushed into production. Seventy-eight of the T28E1s would become part of the U.S. Army contribution to Operation Torch in November 1942. As the U.S. Army did not have air superiority in North Africa, the T28E1 proved a useful addition to the inventory.

In a U.S. Army report on the fighting in North Africa appears this passage on the effectiveness of the T28E1 in battle:

"The proficiency of this mobile weapon can be attributed to three characteristics: Its mobility, enabling it to work well in close support of combat troops in forward area and to patrol roads over which heavy traffic must travel under constant threat of bombing and strafing; its flexible firepower, combining the volume of calibre .50 with the knockdown power of the 37mm; and the facility which the fire is controlled, by using the tracer stream of one calibre .50 to bring it on the target before opening fire with the full volume of its armament. Numerous cases are cited in which a 'mouse trap' effect has been obtained when enemy planes came in much closer on the initial .50 calibre fire than they would on light cannon fire and are caught by the 37mm."

To hasten the fielding of another half-track-based anti-aircraft vehicle the decision came about to improve the T28E1. That upgraded vehicle became the MGMC M15 in October 1942. It retained the Combination Gun Mount M42 from the T28E1. Production of the M15 began in February 1942 and continued until April 1942 with 600 units completed. The vehicle's two 30-gallon petrol tanks resided at the centre of the vehicle, with one located directly behind the driver's compartment, and the second behind and below that.

Major external changes between the T28E1 and the MGMC M15 included the addition of an open-topped, three-sided armoured shield for the gunner, loader, and lead-setter of the M15. The two water-cooled .50-calibre machine guns located above the 37mm automatic cannon of the T28E1 disappeared. On the M15 there appeared two air-cooled .50-calibre machine guns positioned below the barrel of the 37mm automatic cannon barrel.

The positive impression the T28E1 made on the U.S. Army in North Africa led to a requirement for additional anti-aircraft-based half-tracks. As there were no more M42 combination gun mounts available, this led to another model designated as the Combination Gun Mount M54 for fitting onto the modified chassis of a Half-track Personnel Carrier M3. This version of the vehicle became the MGMC M15A1 in September 1943, with Autocar building 1,652 units between October 1943 and February 1944. A total of 100 units of the M15A1 went to the Red Army under Lend-Lease.

Every U.S. Army armoured division by 1944 had a corps-, or army-level attached anti-aircraft artillery (AAA) weapons battalion with a TO&E which called for 32 of the M16s and 32 of the M15/M15A1s.

The secondary mission of the AAA weapons battalions attached to armoured or infantry divisions involved their employment against enemy ground targets ranging from infantry to lightly armoured vehicles, such as armoured cars. Reflected their perceived uselessness, some of the 37mm anti-tank guns mounted on the M6s in North Africa were remounted onto 2nd Armoured Division Half-track Car M2s. The thought was that the vehicle combination was more survivable on the battlefield than the authorized M6.

With continuing demand for additional units of the Multiple Gun Motor Carriage (MGMC) M15, a redesigned pilot seen here appeared with the designation M15E1. The air-cooled .50-calibre machine guns were switched to a position below the 37mm automatic cannon, the opposite of the M15. In this configuration, the M15E1 became the M15A1. *TACOM*

Seeking out anti-aircraft weapons with greater range and knock-down power than the .50-calibre machines of the Multiple Gun Motor Carriage (MGMC) M16, the U.S. Army removed the four .50-calibre machine guns of the M45 mount and replaced them with two 20mm automatic cannons as seen in this picture. The chassis is that of a Half-track Car M2. *TACOM*

A close-up view of the 37mm automatic cannon and two air-cooled .50-calibre machine guns on a Multiple Gun Motor Carriage (MGMC) M15. The improvements that appeared with the introduction of the M15A1 included a lower silhouette that in turn made the vehicle a more stable weapon platform. *National Archives*

In Service and in Action

Early Encounters

The initial combat employment of the new half-tracks in U.S. Army service occurred in the Far East. A total of 46 half-tracks were shipped to the Philippines before the attack on Pearl Harbor. They formed part of the equipment inventory of the Provisional Tank Group, composed of two U.S. Army National Guard tank companies.

Once engaged in action with the invading Japanese Army in December 1941, radio reports from the Provisional Tank Group indicated that the half-tracks experienced numerous mechanical and suspension system problems. Some were traced to the inexperience of the personnel maintaining the vehicles. Some of the valid complaints emanating from the Philippines resulted in changes on the production lines for new-built half-tracks.

In August 1942, the U.S.M.C. 75mm GMC M3s on Guadalcanal engaged in a rare encounter with Japanese tanks. The self-propelled 75s destroyed 11 of the tanks and the leading tank sank in the river trying to escape.

Due to the dearth of Japanese tanks in the Pacific Theatre of Operation the U.S.M.C.'s inventory of the 75mm GMC M3s primarily saw employment as self-propelled artillery. By the last year of the Second World War, the 75mm GMC M3 would find itself replaced in the U.S.M.C. by a more suitable full-tracked self-propelled howitzer, i.e., the M7B1 armed with a 105mm howitzer.

In November 1942, with the Allied military invasion of French North Africa (Operation Torch), the U.S. Army contribution included four tank destroyer battalions equipped with the 75mm GMC M3. They consisted of a headquarters and headquarters company, a reconnaissance company, three gun companies comprised of three platoons each, plus a medical detachment. On paper, each tank destroyer battalion was to have 18 self-propelled anti-aircraft-based half-tracks, although these were not ready in time for all tank destroyer battalions taking part in Operation Torch.

Each gun company of the tank destroyer battalions had three platoons of four self-propelled guns each, for a total of 36 guns within the battalion. Total manpower came out to approximately 900 men. Of the three gun companies in the tank destroyer battalions shipped to North Africa, one platoon, classified as 'light', possessed four units of the 37mm GMC M6.

The M6s were unarmoured 4x4 trucks armed with a shield-mounted 37mm anti-tank gun. The other two platoons in each gun company had the 'heavy' 75mm GMC M3, adding up to 24 units of the 75mm GMC M3 in a tank destroyer battalion. In November 1942, the M6 was pulled from stateside tank destroyer battalions and replaced by the 75mm GMC M3.

1942 Armoured Division

The March 1942 U.S. Army armoured division TO&E called for a total of 604 half-tracks. This number was further broken down into 163 units of the M2, 441 M3s, and 27 of the 81mm Mortar Carrier M4.

There were 77 half-tracks in each of the division's two armoured (tank) regiments. The division's three armoured field artillery battalions had 39 half-tracks each, and the single armoured engineer battalion 46 half-tracks. Some of the half-tracks in the

Right: In this private collector's Half-track Car M3, the Pedestal Truck Mount M25 armed with a dummy .50-calibre machine gun is visible. The machine-gun carriage attaches to a rotatable pintle, which in turn fits into the socket at the top of the pedestal body, and is locked in place with a clamping screw. *Ian Wilcox*

Far right: In this photo taken from over the upper left-hand side of the driver's compartment, we see the troop compartment of a Half-track Personnel Carrier M3. In the centre is the Pedestal Truck Mount M25 on which is mounted a .30-calibre air-cooled machine gun. *Patton Museum*

March 1942 armoured division TO&E also appeared in much smaller numbers divided among the signals company, division train, and the medical company.

Two hundred and thirty of the half-tracks in the March 1942 armoured division TO&E belonged to the division's single armoured infantry regiment, which had three armoured infantry battalions assigned. Each battalion oversaw three armoured infantry companies of 17 half-tracks each, as well as a service and battalion headquarters and battalion headquarters company with another 18 half-tracks: divided among a heavy .30-calibre machine-gun platoon of three half-tracks, an assault gun platoon of seven half-tracks, and a mortar platoon of four half-tracks. The headquarters section, the reconnaissance platoon, and the maintenance section each had one half-track.

The three armoured infantry companies were subdivided into three platoons with five half-tracks each, one of those an M2 for the light .30-calibre machine gun squad of each armoured infantry platoon. The other four would be the M3, one of which transported the platoon's 60mm mortar and crew. The remaining two M3 half-tracks of an armoured infantry company resided in the company headquarters, along with a single 4x4 ¼-ton truck (Jeep).

The term 'light' in reference to .30-calibre machine gun meant it was air-cooled. When the term 'heavy; was employed it described a water-cooled .30-calibre machine gun. Water-cooled provided a machine gun a degree of sustained fire that the air-cooled model could not match.

Authorized armament for the M3 platoon leader vehicle was a .50-calibre vehicular machine gun. It was affixed to either the M25 or M32 pedestal mount, bolted to the floor in the centre of the vehicle. Also, there would be a .30-calibre machine gun on a pintle mount.

Instead of the .50-calibre vehicular machine gun found on platoon leader's vehicles, the other four-half-tracks in an armoured infantry platoon were supposed to have only a .30-calibre vehicular machine gun on a pedestal mount. However, in practice, many half-track crews seem to have preferred arming their vehicles with a pedestal-mounted .50-calibre vehicular machine gun. As with the platoon leader's vehicle, the other four half-tracks in the platoon would also have a .30-calibre machine gun on a pintle mount.

In each armoured infantry platoon, one half-track towed a 37mm Gun M3A1. One of the two armoured infantry company headquarters' half-tracks also towed a 37mm anti-tank gun. In support of each armoured infantry company were three 81mm Mortar Carrier M4s, for a total of nine in the single armoured infantry regiment of the March 1942 armoured division TO&E.

Criticized for their thin armour and lack of overhead protection North Africa servicemen referred to them as 'Purple Heart Boxes'.

A Half-track Personnel Carrier M3A1 appears in this picture. The squad leader sat in the right front seat, operating the .50-calibre machine gun when necessary until disembarking. The assistant squad leader typically sat on the rear left seat (in the troop compartment) and would lead the squad's riflemen out the rear door. *Patton Museum*

Major General Ernest N. Harmon, eventually commander of the 1st Armoured Division, identified the need for more armoured infantry in the March 1942 armoured division TO&E, in a report he submitted in the summer of 1943, but at the same time expressed his disdain for the half-tracks they rode into battle.

Major General Jacob L. Devers, appointed commander of the Armoured Force in August 1941, wrote to Chief of Staff of the Army, General George C. Marshall, that based on his observations of the fighting in North Africa, the half-tracks were ineffective as troop carriers.

Misplaced Doctrine

As the feared hordes of German tanks didn't materialized in North Africa until early 1943, it proved rare indeed for senior officers to hold their attached tank destroyer battalions idle behind the frontlines as tank destroyer doctrine favoured. The 75mm GMC M3s therefore found themselves pressed into frontline service in some unintended roles, "...such as infantry accompanying guns, assault artillery operating with tanks, and in cordon defense instead of depth."

An example of the misuse of 75mm GMC M3-equipped tank destroyer battalions occurred on November 22, 1942. Company B, of the 701st Tank Destroyer Battalion, in complete disregard of accepted tank destroyer doctrine, received orders to capture an enemy-held town. So, without any supporting arms, the company commander ordered his unit to shoot their way into the town. To the surprise of everybody, it succeeded, and the Axis defenders quickly surrendered. The 75mm GMC M3s then went on to ambush an Italian tank column that same day, destroying four without the loss of any of the tank destroyers. The next day Company B, of the 701st Tank Destroyer Battalion, captured 400 Axis soldiers and claimed to have destroyed 11 additional Italian tanks.

The only major large-scale engagement between U.S. Army tank destroyer battalions and German tanks in North Africa occurred on March 23, 1943, at a location known as El Guettar. Fifty advancing German tanks of the 10th Panzer Division, and supporting units, found themselves confronted by the 601st Tank Destroyer Battalion, equipped with the 75mm GMC M3, and a company of 3-inch Gun Motor Carriage (GMC) M10s from the 899th Tank Destroyer Battalion.

When the battle of El Guettar concluded, the German armour advance ended with 30 of their tanks destroyed. U.S. Army losses totalled 20 of the 28 75mm GMC M3s present, and seven of the M10s lost.

With the invasion of Sicily in July 1943, the 75mm GMC M3 had already begun to disappear from frontline service with U.S. Army tank destroyer battalions, as more of the M10s arrived. By the time of the Allied invasion of Italy in September 1943, almost all the half-tracked based tank destroyers were replaced by M10s.

Each armoured infantry rifle platoon had five half-tracks, one of which was supposed to be a Half-track Car M2A1 as pictured. It transported the platoon's light machine-gun squad which, armed with a single .50-calibre machine gun and two dismountable .30-calibre machine guns was meant to support the rifle squads when on foot. *National Archives*

There were no metal enclosures at the bottom rear of the Half-track Personnel Carrier M3/M3A1 as appeared on the Half-track Car M2/M2A1. Instead, the taillights and a covered electrical outlet were recessed into the bottom rear of the troop compartment as pictured. *Pierre Olivier Buan*

Late in the war, as German resistance began to crumble, armoured infantry units without tank support would sometimes drive directly into enemy positions on their half-tracks rather than dismounting and then advancing. There was full awareness that fire from moving half-tracks was extremely inaccurate. However, the shock effect of the half-tracks and the passengers firing all their weapons at close range was sometimes all that was needed to push already demoralized enemy troops into surrendering or fleeing.

The lessons learned in combat by the U.S. Army during its time in North Africa resulted in dramatic adjustments to the TO&E of its armoured divisions. In September 1943, there appeared a new armoured division TO&E, slightly refined with a new armoured division TO&E introduced in February 1944.

Fourteen of the U.S. Army's 16 wartime armoured divisions were eventually converted into the February 1944 TO&E and unofficially referred to as 'light armoured divisions'. Two would retain a modified form of the March 1942 TO&E and be unofficially labelled as 'heavy armoured divisions', reflecting their larger vehicle count.

The number of M2s and M3s in the February 1944 armoured division TO&E was 448, with the majority now being the M3A1 configuration equipped with the armoured M49 ring mount. The M2A1 would by this time be reserved for special duties, such as towing anti-tank guns.

1944 Armoured Division

In the September 1943 and February 1944 U.S. Army armoured division TO&E, the three tank battalions each had 13 half-tracks assigned. The division's reconnaissance squadron was provided with 32 half-tracks, with another 30 in each of the division's three armoured artillery battalions. The armoured division's other half-tracks in smaller numbers resided in the signals company, the division train, medical company, ordnance maintenance battalion, and a single half-track for the military police platoon.

Almost half of the February 1944 TO&E armoured division's half-tracks, a total of 216, were equally divided among the division's three armoured infantry battalions. As with the March 1942 armoured division TO&E, each of the three armoured infantry battalions in the February 1944 armoured division TO&E, was comprised of three rifle companies, a service company, and the battalion headquarters and battalion headquarters' company.

As with the March 1942 armoured division TO&E, the headquarters and battalion headquarters company of the February 1944 armoured division TO&E

oversaw an 81mm mortar platoon, a reconnaissance platoon, a maintenance section, an assault gun platoon, and a heavy .30-calibre machine gun platoon. In time, the howitzer-armed half-tracks of the March 1942 armoured division TO&E disappeared to be replaced by a full-tracked self-propelled howitzer, i.e., the 75mm Howitzer Motor Carriage (HMC) M8.

The primary role of the three armoured infantry battalions in a February 1944 armoured division TO&E was to work in conjunction with its three tank battalions. Among their many assignments were following a tank attack to wipe out remaining enemy resistance, seizing and holding terrain gained by tanks and attacking and seizing terrain favourable for a tank attack. Other tasks included clearing minefield lanes and breaching obstacles with or without engineering support. When required, armoured infantry would form raiding parties to capture enemy prisoners for intelligence-gathering, for example.

On the offensive, tank battalions normally led the armoured infantry battalions. When confronted by strong enemy anti-tank defences, terrain unfavourable for tanks, or an urban area or thick woods inhabited by enemy troops, the armoured infantry battalions would take the lead. The armoured infantry battalions also found themselves tasked with supporting roles for the tank battalions, such as providing security on the march, in assembly areas, and at rallying points. Another role involved guarding nighttime tank bivouac areas.

The three rifle companies of an armoured infantry battalion, in the February 1944 armoured division TO&E, were authorized 20 units of the M3A1. In the February 1944 armoured division TO&E the single 37mm Gun M3A1 anti-tank guns found in each rifle platoon of the March 1942 armoured division TO&E were replaced with a separate anti-tank platoon attached at company level.

The separate anti-tank platoon of the February 1944 armoured division TO&E consisted of three M2A1s, each towing a 57mm Gun M1. Pictorial evidence indicates that among some units M3/M3A1s where pressed into service as towing vehicles for the 57mm anti-tank gun.

Unfortunately, the 57mm anti-tank gun was already obsolete when it entered service. Firing an armour-piercing (AP) projectile at a muzzle velocity of 2,800 feet per second, in theory it could penetrate 79mm of armour at 1,000 yards. In some armoured divisions in the ETO the 57mm anti-tank guns were discarded, and their gun crews re-purposed as armoured infantrymen.

Of the five half-tracks in the armoured infantry rifle platoon of the March 1944 armoured division TO&E, three carried a rifle squad of 12 men. One of the other two half-tracks transported two dismountable .30-calibre light (air-cooled) machine guns with their crews and tripods. The other provided transportation for an eight-man crew armed with a dismountable 60mm mortar. It was not unheard of for armoured infantry rifle platoons to acquire additional 60mm mortars.

The three rifle squads of an armoured infantry rifle platoon, at full-strength,

This privately owned Half-track Personnel Carrier M3 has the factory-built luggage racks on either side of the rear door, which appeared as from September 1943 for the M2/M3 half-track series. Besides providing additional storage space for the vehicle's crew, the racks were intended to store the vehicle's winterization kit. *Pierre Oliver Buan*

On the M3/M3A1 pictured, the rear door is blocked by an improvised storage rack and cargo. Ease of access was less important than stowage space. *National Archives*

In this picture, we see a Half-track Personnel Carrier M3 as the prime mover for a 3-inch anti-tank gun. The concept of towed anti-tank guns also proved to be badly conceived. *National Archives*

consisted of a squad leader (sergeant) who also acted as the vehicle commander, an assistant squad leader (corporal), nine riflemen, and a driver. The driver would typically have a sub-machine gun.

Depending on the situation, the M3/M3A1 driver might remain with his half-track in a nearby defensive position awaiting the order to retrieve the other members of the rifle squad. On other occasions, he might take part in dismounted actions. The rifle squad leader could also assign the vehicular machine guns on the M3/M3A1 to one of the squad's riflemen to fire in support of his dismounted comrades.

As the U.S. Army's armoured infantry battalions in the armoured divisions were in the forefront of fighting, the vehicles were subjected to a wide range of enemy weapons included mines of varying sizes. Here a mine has destroyed the right front suspension unit of this Half-track Personnel Carrier M3A1. *National Archives*

Mud proved to be a significant problem from the fall of 1944 up through the early months of 1945 as seen with this Half-track Car M2A1. In anticipation of such issues and the adverse impact on off-road mobility of the M2/M3 series half-tracks, the army decided in August 1942 that track chains were a better choice than grousers (track extensions). *National Archives*

Of the nine riflemen assigned to an M3/M3A1, one would find himself assigned as the assistant driver. He would sit in the middle seat of the forward compartment, with the driver on his left, and the squad leader on his right. Another rifleman had the job of carrying the Launcher, Rocket, Anti-tank, 2.36 Inch, M1 or M9/M9A1 (bazooka). The soldier carrying it into battle received the name 'rocketeer'. Another rifleman acted as his loader.

From a 1943-dated U.S. Army manual titled *Armoured Command: Crew Drills for Half-Track Vehicles* is this passage on what the rocketeer and was supposed to do before disembarking from his vehicle: "Assembles rocket launcher; puts on ammunition bag with three rockets handed to him by the loader; checks electrical firing mechanism; resumes mounted post holding launcher in his hands. He leaves his rifle in its scabbard while prepared for action as rocketeer."

The same manual goes on to describe what the rocketeer's loader would do upon being ordered by the squad leader to dismount from the vehicle: "Removes two ammunition bags and six rockets from stowage place; hands one bag and three rockets to rocketeer; puts on bag with three rockets; resumes mounted post holding rifle in his hands."

All of the weapons on board rifle squad half-tracks could be fired from within the vehicle, including the rocket launcher. However, this could only take place when approved by the squad leader. In contrast to regular U.S. Army infantry squads of 12 men, one man had a Browning automatic rifle (BAR), whereas the half-track-based rifle squad had no BAR. They depended on the light (air-cooled) .30-calibre machine-gun squad assigned to one of the platoon's five half-tracks, or the heavy (water cooled) .30-calibre machine-gun platoon of the armoured infantry battalion headquarters for firepower support in battle. In spite of this, armoured infantrymen often added BARs to their inventory of weapons.

To increase passenger safety in M2/M3 troop compartments when travelling cross-country, internal hand grips were authorized in February 1943, on all newly built vehicles as well as those in the field. In March 1944, the addition of luggage racks on the external rear vertical plates of both the M2 and M3 was approved. Some M2/M3 crews had improvised a wide variety of luggage rack/boxes on the back of vehicles.

Issues

Armoured infantrymen suffered some of the highest casualty rates in the ETO, with never enough trained replacements available. In some cases, the shortage of armoured infantrymen meant that besides anti-tank crews turned into armoured infantrymen, 60mm mortar team crews were reassigned.

From a wartime U.S. Army report by the medical corps comes this passage regarding the problem of armoured infantrymen seeing too much combat:

"In armored divisions, with too few armored infantry, the infantry contributes from 80 to 90 percent of the combat exhaustion casualties, rates becoming extremely high after the third or fifth days of action. In hard, continued action, armored infantry companies may be down to 40–50 men (out of a strength of 245), with three company commanders casualties in the process. One unit had 150–180 percent replacements in 200 days; another had 100 percent turnover in 60–70 days."

At times, armoured divisions had to borrow footborne infantry battalions from nearby infantry divisions for certain missions due to the high losses among their armoured infantry battalions or requiring more infantrymen than found in the armoured infantry battalions. As the standard footborne infantry battalions lacked half-tracks, the armoured division would provide 2½-ton 6x6 trucks from the armoured division's inventory.

The problem with employing footborne infantry battalions in the role of armoured infantry is they were unfamiliar with the much quicker tempo of operations, lacked the training for combined-arms assault, and lacked the close association that armoured infantry battalions had with their tank battalion counterparts, whom they fought alongside.

Late War Impressions

Found within the March 1945 U.S. Army report is a passage by Lieutenant Colonel R. W. Jenna, commanding 41st Armored Infantry Regiment, 2nd Armored Division, who mentions a couple of design features found on the German SdKfz. 251 series of armoured half-track personnel carriers that he would have liked to have seen on U.S. Army half-tracks: "A well-protected air scoop and radiator vent so that the panel in front of the radiator core could be completely and permanently sealed with armour plate. This would reduce radiator casualties by a great percentage."

Jenna, like others who had a chance to test captured German armoured personnel carrier half-tracks, went on in the March 1945 report to describe some of the advantages the American half-tracks possessed over their enemy counterparts. In his opinion, these included the American half-track suspension system and band tracks that provided their crews "much better riding quality and more silent operation".

He went on to state that the power plant and the powertrain of the American half-tracks were far superior to those on their German counterparts, reporting they had a higher level of on-road mobility, as well as off-road mobility in a wider variety of terrain.

The Free French Army crew of this Half-track Personnel Carrier M3 have added chains to the band tracks, but not the front wheels. The chains employed on the M2/M3 series half-tracks were of conventional construction and built of standard tyre chain material. *National Archives*

Pictured is the crew of a Half-track Personnel Carrier M3 who arrayed around the exterior of their vehicle an extensive range of equipment and no doubt personal gear. Standard practice called for the soldiers to leave their vehicles immediately upon encountering the enemy and entering into combat on foot. *National Archives*

In wartime a 12-man rifle squad was usually carried on board a Half-track Personnel Carrier M3/M3A1, all were equipped with the M1 Garand rifles except the driver who had a sub-machine gun. *Chun-lun Hsu*

The problem with the poor off-road mobility of the half-tracks, especially in mud, compared to tanks appears in an after-action report of the 5th Armored Division in the ETO during March 1945:

"The terrain greatly hampered the operation. Although flat and slightly rolling and giving the appearance of being firm it bogged down all the half-tracks behind the tanks. One company attempted to attack towing the half-tracks behind the tanks, but this proved unsatisfactory, and the operation was concluded with the infantry riding on the decks of the tanks." In the same report an officer of the 5th Armored Division stated the following: "In heavy going do not trust half-tracks. Put infantry and their supporting weapons on tank decks. A long rope on [the] tank is useful for dismounted infantry to hold onto."

This Half-track Car M2A1 lost its right front wheel to a German mine. Notice the very large improvised wooden storage container on the rear of the vehicle, which more than likely started out as a shipping crate. *Patton Museum*

There was a shortage of Multiple Gun Motor Carriage (MGMC) M16s during the Korean War. The U.S. Army issued a contract to convert over 1,500 units of the Half-track Personnel Carrier M3 into the vehicle seen here designated the M16A1. Notice the lack of folding-down armour flaps around the troop compartment. *TACOM*

Post-war Employment

With the outbreak of the Korean War in 1950, the U.S. Army quickly started to gather whatever useful equipment it could find for deployment to that theatre of conflict. In its stockpiles in occupied Japan were some M15A1s and M16s. As there proved to be a shortage of 37mm ammunition, the decision was made to replace the existing weapons and carriage on the M15A1 with a single 40mm automatic cannon. In this new configuration, the vehicle became the 40mm GMC M34.

Upon arrival in South Korea, small locally fabricated fixed armour plates began appearing on either side of the M45D four-gun mount of the M16. The reason was to protect the two standing loaders on its rear platform. The added armour on these vehicles became known as 'bat wings'.

As the M16 proved to be a much-in-demand weapon in Korea and there were not enough in the inventory, the American firm of Bowen & McLaughlin received a U.S. Army contract to convert 1,662 units of the Half-track Personnel Carrier M3 into a modified version of the M16. These converted vehicles became the M16A1 in April 1952. Unlike the M16, the M16A1 retained the rear door of the M3.

To provide clearance over the sides and rear of the M16A1, as the converted M3s lacked the folding armour flaps of the M16, the M45D four-gun mount sat on an even taller extension ring than that fitted in the M16. With this arrangement, the M45D became the M45F. The latter also had applied at the factory folding armour plates, i.e., bat wings on either side of the M45F to protect the two standing loaders. Eventually, the existing M16s received the changes applied to the M16A1, including the rear door, and became the M16A2 in May 1953.

Despite the poor off-road mobility of the Second World War vintage half-tracks, they still packed a powerful punch on the battlefields of Korea. The usefulness of the anti-aircraft half-tracks would keep them in service following the Korean War with the U.S. Army until 1958. The bulk of the Second World War-vintage half-tracks models remaining in the U.S. Army's inventory found themselves declared obsolete prior to the Korean War and pulled from service.

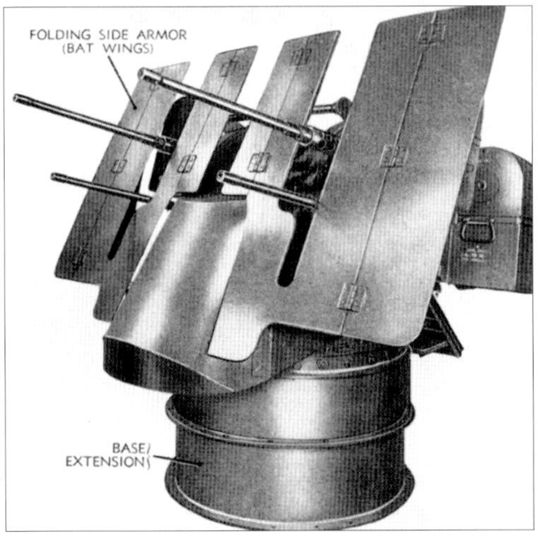

To provide enough clearance for the quad .50 Calibre Machine Gun Mount M45D to rotate and depress on the Multiple Gun Motor Carriage (MGMC) M16A1 an extension at the bottom was added as shown. In this configuration, it became the M45F. To protect the loaders (cannoneers) standing on the rear platform of the M45F, the factory-made armoured shield appeared. *TACOM*